God's grace is the only grace,
And all grace is the grace of God.

A BOOK OF GRACES

compiled by

CAROLYN MARTIN

Illustrations by
Bert Wharton

HODDER AND STOUGHTON
W.I. BOOKS LTD

The grace on page 1 is from Coventry Patmore, *The Angel in the House*, submitted by Richard Baker O.B.E.

British Library Cataloguing in Publication Data

A book of graces.
  1. Grace at meals
  I. Martin, Carolyn
242'.8   BV283.G7

ISBN 0 340 25761 x

PREFACE

The saying of grace pre-dates Christianity. The history of graces can be traced back to Greek and Roman literature and then from the Old and the New Testament to the writings of the early Christian fathers. Evidence of pre-Reformation graces comes from the rules laid down by religious communities and the first official primers or prayer books with graces, in Britain, were issued during the reign of Henry VIII. After the 1560's there were few officially approved primers and the initiative was left to private individuals or poets. This is still the practice today.

The word grace comes from the latin *gratias*, meaning thanks. Originally this was translated as graces, but by the sixteenth century the word was shortened to grace—possibly because graces was thought to refer to the prayers before and after a meal. Today, saying grace in private homes has largely lapsed, apart from more formal occasions. Many colleges, London Livery Companies and other organizations however still have their own graces.

This collection is an attempt to set down some of the forms of grace used in the past and those in use today, both in this country and abroad. Some graces have been chosen for their function and others for their poetry and lyrical qualities. It is worth noting that this particular form of thanksgiving has been responsible for some of our most profound and beautiful verse. Many of the graces have not been published before and, as well as being a useful handbook, I hope that the collection will serve as an example of social history and a mirror of contemporary society. Perhaps it will also be of some help to those who are asked to say grace and can think of nothing more inspiring to say than 'For what we are about to receive...'

ACKNOWLEDGMENTS

The following graces are the result of my own researches and letters from many correspondents—some individually approached and others from open letters in magazines and journals. I must thank all these correspondents, to whom I have tried to give due acknowledgment. The name of the person who first brought the grace to my attention, is placed after the grace, in italics. Finally, I must thank my husband for his assiduous help and encouragement and my children for their patience.

Carolyn Martin
Clocaenog 1980

CONTENTS

I

Literary Graces

Although not graces as such, many of the following quotations refer to the practice of saying grace, without giving the actual form or words. These have been included to illustrate the history of graces through the centuries.

Homer *Iliad* VII 480

> Nor did anyone dare to drink till he had made
> libation to Zeus All-mighty.

Virgil 70–19 B.C. *Aeneid* V 62–63

> Invite we then, the feast to grace,
> The home-gods of our own proud race,
> And those our host reveres.

Clement of Alexandria A.D. 150–213, a Father of the Greek Church. *Paedagogus* A.D. 190

> It is meet before we partake of food to bless
> the maker of all things, and to sing when drinking.

St. Basil 330–79. One of the three Cappadocian Fathers and a brilliant leader of philosophical Christian orthodoxy in the late fourth century.

> Before meat let grace be said . . .
> say grace after meat in gratitude for gifts given.

St. Chrysostom 347–407. Bishop of Constantinople and 'Doctor of the Church'—a title given to Christian theologians of outstanding merit. St. Chrysostom gives a prayer used after their meal by the Eastern monks of the desert.

Blessed God, who feedest me from my youth up, who givest food to all flesh, fill our hearts with joy and gladness, that always having all sufficiency, we may abound unto every good work in Jesus Christ our Lord, with whom be unto thee glory, honour and might, with the Holy Spirit for ever.

The Bayeux Tapestry 1070–80. The tapestry is an embroidered strip of linen, about eighty yards long and nineteen inches wide. It was probably commissioned by Bishop Odo of Bayeux and was made in Kent. It depicts the events leading up to and including the Norman Conquest. In section 51, Bishop Odo says grace by blessing the food and drink.

> 51. Et hic Episcopus cibum et potum benedicit.
> Odo Episcopus: Willelm: Rotbert: Iste.

William Langland 1330?–1400? in *The Vision of Piers Plowman* XV 326, quotes several passages from the Bible as graces. Psalm 112, v. 9.

> He hath dispersed, he hath given to the poor;
> His righteousness endureth for ever.

Geoffrey Chaucer 1345–1400. 'The Tale of Melibee' v. 2990.

> they weren right glad and joyful, and answereden ful mekely and benignely/yeldynge graces and thankynges to hir Lord Melibee and to al his compaignye.

Fabliau of Sir Cleyes *c.* 1450. A fabliau is a short tale in French verse, often dealing with incidents in everyday life from a comic point of view.

> But whether we have less or more
> Always thank we God therefore.

Thomas à Kempis 1380–1471. An Augustinian monk from Germany, whose writings included the famous *Imitation of Christ*.

> Be thankful for the least gift,
> So shalt thou be meet to receive the greater.

Desiderius Erasmus 1466–1536. 'The Profane Feast' in *Familiar Colloquies of Erasmus*, translated by N. Bailey, 1877.

> May he that feeds all Things with his Bounty command his Blessing upon what is or shall be set upon this table.

William Shakespeare 1564–1616

King Henry VI Part II, Act I, Scene I.

> King Henry: O Lord, that lends me life,
>   Lend me a heart replete with thankfulness!

Macbeth Act III, Scene IV.

> Macbeth: Now, good digestion wait on appetite,
>   and health on both.

The Taming of the Shrew, Act IV, Scene I.

Petruchio: Come, Kate sit down; I know you have a
stomach.
   Will you give thanks, sweet Kate; or else shall I?

Ben Jonson 1572–1637. Dramatist, poet and critic. The
grace is a typical example of Jonson's humour and fearless
honesty. From the life of Ben Jonson in Aubrey's *Brief Lives*,
published in 1898.

A Grace by Ben Jonson extempore before King James

Our King and Queen the Lord-God blesse,
The Paltzgrave and the Lady Besse,
And God blesse every living thing
That lives, and breath's, and loves the King.
God bless the Councell of Estate,
And Buckingham the fortunate.
God Blesse them all, and keepe them safe:
And God Blesse me, and God blesse Raph.

The King was mighty enquisitive to know who this
Raph was. Ben told him 'twas the Drawer at the
Swanne Tavernne by Charing cross, who drew him
good Canarie. For this Drollery his Majestie gave him
an hundred poundes.

C. M. Mowll, Clerk to the Clothworkers' Company

John Dryden 1631–1700. One of the greatest literary
figures of his age, excelling in both prose and verse. Prologue
to *Caesar Borgia* 42.

But mark their feasts ... The Pope says grace,
but 'tis the Devil gives thanks.

Joseph Addison 1672–1719. Famous for his *Coverley Essays*, contributed to *The Spectator*. Addison censures the false modesty of the English gentleman for not saying grace. *The Spectator*, 458, Friday 15th August 1712.

> Our excess of Modesty makes us shame-faced in all the Exercises of Piety and Devotion. This Humour prevails upon us daily; insomuch that at many well-bred Tables, the Master of the House is so very Modest a Man, that he has not the Confidence to say Grace at his own Table: A Custom which is not only practised by all the Nations about us, but was never omitted by the Heathens themselves.

Dr. Samuel Johnson 1709–84. *Anecdotes of the Late Samuel Johnson* by Hester Lynch Piozzi (Piozzi was Hester Thrale's name by her second marriage.)

An Anecdote by Hester Thrale

When talking to his friend Hester Thrale, Dr. Johnson told her that he and his wife Tetty would sometimes quarrel at the dinner table when he was saying grace. He quoted his wife as saying,

'Nay hold, Mr. Johnson, and do not make a farce of thanking God for a dinner which in a few minutes you will protest not eatable.'

G. W. Nicholls, Ph.D., Curator of the Samuel Johnson Birthplace Museum, Lichfield, Staffs., who comments that a Book of Graces would have appealed to Dr. Johnson, bringing together two things very dear to him—religion and eating.

William Cowper 1731–1800. A thanksgiving for food in one of his Olney Hymns, *Grace and Providence*, No 46:

Almighty King! Whose wondrous hand
Supports the weight of sea and land,
Whose Grace is such a boundless store,
No heart shall break that sighs for more.

Thy Providence supplies my food,
And 'tis thy Blessing makes it good;
My soul is nourished by Thy Word,
Let soul and body praise the Lord.

Charles Lamb 1775–1834. An extract from 'Grace before Meat' in *The Essays of Elia*, 1823.

Would you have Christians sit down at table, like hogs to their troughs, without remembering the Giver?—no—I would have them sit down as Christians, remembering the Giver, and less like hogs. Or if their appetites must run riot, and they must pamper themselves with delicacies for which east and west are ransacked, I would have them postpone their benediction to a fitter season, when appetite is laid; when the still small voice can be heard, and the reason of the grace

17

returns—with temperate diet and restricted dishes. Gluttony and surfeiting are no proper occasions for thanksgiving.

Charles Dickens 1812–1870. Dickens was not attracted by the ritual aspect of Christianity and as far as it known, he did not have a grace of his own. In *Oliver Twist* he mentions '*a long grace was said over the short commons*'. There is a burlesque grace put into the mouth of Mr. Chadband in *Bleak House*, Ch. 19:

'My friends' says Mr. Chadband, 'we have partaken in moderation' (which was certainly not the case so far as he was concerned), 'of the comforts which have been provided for us. May this house live upon the fatness of the land; may corn and wine be plentiful therein; may it grow, may it thrive, may it prosper, may it advance, may it proceed, may it press forward!'

A Christmas Dinner from Sketches by Boz

Reflect upon your present blessings, of which every man has many, not upon your past misfortunes, of which all men have some.

Harold Wilshaw, the cookery writer, who adds that this grace would presage an excellent dinner, where there were some present blessings to reflect upon. Other information from the Dickens Fellowship.

William Barnes 1801–1886, the Dorsetshire poet, who published grammars and glossaries of the Dorset dialect. He was rector of Winterbourne Came from 1862 until his death.

> Lord, may we bless thee for these gifts of love
> Our food today, nor deem the gift is small;
> And seek the bread that cometh from above,
> The life-stay of the soul, the best of all.

Alfred Austin 1835–1913. Poet Laureate from 1896. From his *Haunts of Ancient Peace*.

> For these, and all his other mercies, above all the crowning mercy of serious conversation, God's name be praised.

The Rubáiyát of Omar Khayyám, translated by E. FitzGerald and first published in 1859.

> Here with a Loaf of Bread beneath the Bough,
> A Flask of Wine, a Book of Verse—and Thou
>   Beside me singing in the Wilderness—
> And Wilderness is Paradise enow.

James Joyce 1882–1941. It is interesting to note that Joyce uses the traditional Roman Catholic grace in his writings. A grace spoken by Stephen in *Portrait of the Artist as a Young Man*.

> Bless us, O Lord, and these thy gifts which through thy bounty we are about to receive through Christ our Lord. Amen.

Mrs. Jean Jackson

Dame Ivy Compton-Burnett 1892–1969. A grace spoken by Mr. Merry, the Latin teacher, in *Pastors and Masters*.

> For these and all other mercies
> may we be given thankful hearts.

Howard Spring 1889–1965. A grace by Gordon Stansfield in *Fame is the Spur*.

> These mercies bless, and grant that we may feast in Paradise with thee.

Mrs. Celia Lomax

2

16th & 17th Centuries

With the Renaissance and Reformation and the upsurge of interest in religion, many new graces were composed.

Martin Luther 1483–1546

Dominum Jesus sit potus et esus.

Lord Jesus be drink and food.

Other graces attributed to Luther

Come Lord Jesus be our guest,
And may our meal by you be blest. Amen.

Jim Scott, Scargill House, N. Yorks.

Lord Jesus, be with us in this,
as in all things, for your Name's sake.

John Chaplin

Thomas Tallis 1510–85. English organist and composer of church music. Some of his hymn tunes are still in daily use. He was organist at Waltham Abbey until 1540, with the dissolution of the monasteries, but became joint organist, with his pupil Byrd, at the Chapel Royal from 1572. Byrd and Tallis were given the monopoly of music printing for twenty-one years by Elizabeth I.

To God who gives our daily bread
A thankful song we raise,
And pray that he who sends us food
May fill our hearts with praise.

Three Graces by George Bellin, an ironmonger from
Exeter. They are dated 1565. The first grace is widely used
today and was especially popular during the present Queen
Elizabeth's Silver Jubilee year in 1977.

1   God bless our meat,
      God guide our ways,
      God give us grace
      Our Lord to please.
      Lord long preserve in peace and health
      Our gracious Queen Elizabeth.

2   Almighty God, Eternal King
      Which madest heaven and every thing:
      Grant unto us that present be
      To taste the food that here we see.

3   Now we have both meat and drink,
      Our bodies to sustain;
      Let us remember helpless folk,
      Whom need doth cause to pine.
      And like as God is merciful
      To us giving such store;
      So let us now be pitiful
      In helping of the poor.
      Then shall we find it true indeed
      God will forsake us never,
      But help us when we have most need,
      To whom be praise for ever. Amen.

The duty of saying grace is officially recognized in the Primers or Prayer Books issued during the reigns of Henry VIII, Edward VI and Elizabeth I.

1536 Primer of Salisbury use

> Good Lord for thy Grace meekly we call,
> Bless us and our meals and drinks withal;
> In the name of the Father and of the Son
> and of the Holy Ghost. Amen.

1553 Primer or book of private prayer

Grace before meat

> Pray we to God the Almighty Lord
> That sendeth food to beasts and men
> To send his blessing on this board,
> To feed us now and ever. Amen.

Thanks after meat

> Blessed be the Father celestial
> Who hath fed us with his material bread;
> Beseeching him likewise to feed the soul,
> And grant us his kingdom when we be dead.

A Grace from an Elizabethan Primer

> Geve thãks to God with one accord
> For that shalbe set on this borde
> And be not carefull what to eate
> To eche thing liuing the lorde sendes meate
> For foode he will not see you perishe
> But will you feede foster and cherishe
> Take wel in worth that he hath sent ...

1580 An Elizabethan Primer

> Bless these thy gifts most gracious God
> From whom all goodness springs;
> Make clean our hearts and feed our souls
> With good and joyful things.

> *Rev. Dr. Gordon Huelin,*
> *Vicar of St. Margaret Pattens,*
> *Eastcheap*

Robert Herrick 1591–1674. Three poems as graces. The following is one of his best-known verses, although it is doubtful whether it was ever intended as a grace.

> 1   Here a little child I stand
> Heaving up my either hand.
> Cold as paddocks* though they be
> Still I lift them up to thee,
> For a benison to fall
> On our meat and on us all.

> *Paddocks—toads.

Grace for a Child

2 What God gives, and what we take,
'Tis a gift for Christ his sake:
Be the meal of beans and pease,
God be thanked for those and these:
Have we flesh or have we fish
All are fragments from his dish.
He his Church save, and the King,
And our peace here, like a spring,
Make it ever flourishing.

From 'A Thanksgiving for his home'

3   Lord I confess to, when I dine
    The pulse is thine,
    And all those other bits that be
    There placed by thee;
    The worts,* the purslain,* and the mess
    Of water cress,
    Which of thy kindness thou hast sent;
    And my content
    Makes these and my beloved beet,
    To be more sweet.

*Herbs

George Herbert 1593–1633. The first and probably the greatest of the Metaphysical poets.

Thou who hast given so much to me,
Give one thing more, a grateful heart, for Christ's sake.

John Donne 1571–1631. Another of the Metaphysical poets. A Roman Catholic for the early part of his life, Donne took Anglican orders in 1615. As Dean of St. Paul's, from 1621 to his death, he is said to have preached some of the best sermons in the seventeenth century.

May God be praised that all things be so good.

Rev. Canon Edwyn Young

John Milton 1608–74. From his hymn 'Let us with a gladsome mind . . .', from Psalm 136. *(Hymns Ancient and Modern* 377)

> Let us, with a gladsome mind,
> Praise the Lord, for he is kind:
> All things living he doth feed,
> His full hand supplies their need.

A Royalist's Grace during the time of Cromwell, whose name was often pronounced Crumwell.

> God send this crumb well down.

1656 A Grace from 'The Practice of Piety'.

Grace before Meat

> O Lord bless unto our use thy creatures at this time provided for our sustenance, that being preserved hereby and comforted, we may do thee more laudable service unto thy glory, who art the author of all good, through Jesus Christ our Lord. Amen.

Jeremiah Clarke 1669–1707. A Restoration musician and composer for the church and theatre. He committed suicide in a house in St. Paul's churchyard when organist of the cathedral, for the love of a young woman.

> Great God, thou Giver of all good,
> Accept our praise and bless our food:
> Grace, health and strength to us afford
> Through Jesus Christ, our risen Lord.

1671 A Grace from the King's Psalter

O Lord, the merciful and good,
Bless and sanctify our food.
Grant they to us may wholesome be,
And makes us thankful unto thee. Amen.

1699 Grace from 'England's Perfect Schoolmaster', published by Nathaniel Strong.

Grace after Meat

All praise and glory is due to thee, O God, which dost load us continually with thy mercies, and has at this time plentifully fed our vile bodies: we beseech thee to feed our souls with thy precious word, which is the Bread of Life, and make us truly thankful for all thy mercies, for the sake of Jesus Christ our Lord. Amen.

3

London
Livery
Companies

The Livery Companies are guilds of the City of London, many of which were formed during the fourteenth and fifteenth centuries, as urban trade organizations. They earned their name by virtue of their special costume, which distinguished them from the yeomen. Nowadays the Companies have lost almost all of their original industrial functions, although the social activities remain and many administer valuable educational and other charities.

The Laudi Spirituali 1545. A 'Grace after Dinner', sung by many of the London Livery Companies.

> For these and all thy mercies given,
> We bless and praise thy name, O Lord!
> May we receive them with thanksgiving,
> Ever trusting in thy word.
> To thee alone be honour, glory,
> Now and henceforth for evermore. Amen.

The Mercers' Company Grace, composed by the late Very Rev. F. P. Harton, Dean of Wells, when he was Master of the Mercers' Company, 1949–50.

> May God grant us grace and gratitude,
> and vouchsafe alway to dwell with us,
> through Jesus Christ our Lord. Amen.

The Skinners' Company Grace before Meat, composed by a past Master of the Company, Rev. Adam Fox, Archdeacon of Westminster and Sub-Dean of the Abbey. The grace is always said at the Election Night Dinner, held on the Feast of Corpus Christi—the Thursday after Trinity Sunday.

Corpus Christi veneremur et cibum cum immortalem tum mortalem grato animo accipiamus per eundem Christum Dominum nostrum. Amen.

On this the Feast Day of Corpus Christi let us reverence and revere in our hearts the body of Christ; and take and eat both of that spiritual food, and of this earthly bounty, with thankful minds; through the same Christ Jesus our Lord.

Translation by Dr. Walter Oakeshott

The Haberdashers' Company Grace, which has recently been translated into Latin.

Preserve, O Lord, the Church, the Queen and the Worshipful Company of Haberdashers, and bless these gifts to our use and ourselves to thy service. Amen.

Benedic, Domine, quaesumus Ecclesiae sanctae tuae, Reginae nostrae augustissimae, necnon et societati reverendae Haberdasherorum; et concede ut, salubriter his tuis donis enutriti, tibi debitum obsequium praestare valeamus; per Jesum Christum Dominum nostrum. Amen.

The Grocers' Company Grace after Dinner

For these and all his mercies God's Holy Name be blessed and praised; and may God preserve the Church, the Queen, and the Worshipful Company of Grocers.

The Vintners' Company Grace

For these and all his mercies;
God's holy name be praised;
May he preserve the Church and Queen;
And ever prosper this Ancient Mystery of Vintners.

The Merchant Taylors' Company Grace after Dinner

May God give us thankful hearts
and keep us in friendship and brotherly love
to our live's end.

The Waxchandlers' Company Grace before Meat,
written by the Venerable Rennie Simpson, Archdeacon of
Macclesfield, and former Precentor of Westminster Abbey.

For thy creature the Bee,
The Wax and the Honey,
We thank thee, O Lord.

By the light of all men,
Christ Jesus our King,
May this food now be blessed. Amen.

The Clothworkers' Company Graces. The Clothworkers' Company have a unique collection of graces used
by the Company between 1853–63 and preserved by Mr.
C. F. Angell, Master 1858–9. The Laudi Spirituali was the
grace most often used and this is still sung after most Clothworkers' Dinners. The following two graces are from the
collection.

A 'New Grace' composed by Wm Bayley, for the dinner
on 5th July 1854. This was the grace used on 27th March
1860, at the banquet to H.R.H. the Prince Consort for the
inauguration of the new (Victorian) Hall—destroyed 1941.

O Lord, by whom all our wants are supplied,
and from whom cometh every good and perfect gift;
we acknowledge with thankful hearts these and all thy
    mercies.
May we improve them to thy glory, through Jesus Christ
    our Lord. Amen.

A 'New Grace' composed by J. W. Hobbs, for the
dinner on 5th December 1855.

To thee, O God, the mighty Lord, most high,
Who dost our wants with lib'ral hand supply,
Our grateful hearts and voices now we raise,
To heav'n's high throne we chaunt our hymn of praise,
We bless, we praise, we magnify thy name,
Now and henceforth for evermore. Amen.

The Woolmen's Company Graces. It is traditional for the Chaplain of the Company to write a new grace for each dinner. The present Chaplain is the Rev. Neville Barker Cryer. These are some of their many graces.

1　May God, as Shepherd of his sheep,
　　Bless us as Woolmen whilst we eat.
　　And, as his sheep, we safely graze,
　　For bounty thank him, all our days. Amen.

A Grace for the Ladies' Banquet on 22nd June 1978

2　　May God, who first gave Eve to man,
　　　Who made him dig while wool she span,
　　　Grant us to weave at Woolmen's table,
　　　Such webs of friendship as we're able.
　　　And digging into food and wine,
　　　Let us yet bless his name divine.

Grace for All Saints' Day, 1st November, 1978

3　O God our father
　　grant that as, on this special day,
　　we remember with thankfulness
　　those of our Founders and Benefactors
　　who now rejoice at thy heavenly table,
　　so we too may not only rejoice
　　at thy bounties on this table
　　but show our gratitude by good lives
　　lived to thy glory.
　　Through Jesus Christ our Lord.

Grace for Alms Court Dinner, 17th January 1979

4   As amongst tallow-candles tall
    Thanks came from past men in this hall
    So may we, Lord, who now here meet
    Echo their 'grace' for all we eat.

The Glovers' Company Grace for the Mansion Hall Banquet

With warm hands and true hearts
We welcome all to this great Hall,
It is our prayer
As we share
The meats upon our table,
That God may bless each one
And so enable
His will be done,
His Kingdom come
On earth
As it is in Heaven. Amen.

The Scriveners' Company Grace, composed by the Company's Honorary Chaplain, Rev. Peter Lillingston.

God bless this food upon our board
And may thy name be aye adored.
We thank thee for thy gifts assured
By death and resurrection of our Lord.
Hear now, O God, The Scriveners' plea;
That we may ever mindful be
Of those less fortunate than we.
And through these gifts draw nearer Thee. Amen.

The Painter-Stainers' Company Grace

For these and all God's gifts to us,
For our fellowship one with another,
For the good name of this ancient Company,
For the obedience which springs from love,
God's holy name be praised.

The Carpenters' Company Grace

For these, and all His mercies,
We honour God.

The Blacksmiths' Company Grace, composed in 1935 by the Rev. H. Stephenson Payne, who became Prime Warden in 1954. His family have a long tradition of association with the Guild.

For Good Health and Fair Wealth,
Good Food and Good Fellowship,
God's Name be praised.

The Plaisterers' Company Grace

Bless, O Lord before we dine,
Each dish of food, each glass of wine,
And make us evermore aware,
How much, O Lord, we're in thy care.

The Armourers and Brasiers' Company Grace, composed by the Venerable Claud Scott, Archdeacon of Suffolk and a past Master of the Company.

> For good fare and good fellowship,
> praise God.

The Bakers' Company Grace and Motto

> Praise God for all.

The Leathersellers' Company Grace, often used by the Rev. F. J. Dove, a former Honorary Chaplain of the Company.

> For good food provided
> For good health to enjoy it
> For good friends to share it
> Thanks be to God.

A Grace used by the Saddlers' Company

> For good food, good wine and good friends,
> Let us thank God,
> And pray that we do not forget those less
> Fortunate than ourselves.

4

Legal
Graces

Graces used by the Four Inns of Court. The Inns of Court are voluntary societies with the power to call law students to the English Bar. The Inns originated in the thirteenth century and all four have equal privileges; they provide dining halls, libraries and chapels, promote lectures, examine candidates and have the power to disbar members.

GRAY'S INN

Grace before Dinner

Benedic, Domine, nos et haec tua dona quae de bonitate tua sumpturi sumus. Amen.

Bless, O Lord, us and these gifts which by thy goodness we are about to eat.

Grace after Dinner

Agimus tibi gratias, Omnipotens Deus, pro donis tuis, per Jesum Christum, Dominum nostrum. Amen.

Accept for thyself, Almighty God, thanks for thy gifts, through Jesus Christ, our Lord. Amen.

The Rt. Hon. the Lord Edmund-Davies

INNER TEMPLE

The Inner Temple have some interesting manuscripts relating to their graces. In a manuscript dated 1505, the Master of the Temple was asked to say grace. If the Grace Book was not on the board, each butler had to forfeit a penny. This money was to be given to a poor man to pray for the soul of John Nethersole, an early benefactor of the Society. The principal function of the Grace Book was to be banged on the table, as a signal for grace to begin. In order to protect the book from such treatment, in 1932 the

Treasurer ordered that a dummy book of blank leaves should be made, resembling as nearly as possible the original book.

Grace before Dinner	**Grace after Dinner**
Benedictus benedicat.	Benedicto benedicatur.
Let the blessed bless.	Let the blessed be blessed.

The Rt. Hon. the Viscount Dilhorne

LINCOLN'S INN

Grace before Dinner

Bless, O Lord, we beseech thee, these thy creatures to our use, and ourselves to thy service, through Jesus Christ our Lord.

Grace after Dinner

God be praised for all his blessings; God preserve the Queen, the Church, and this Honourable Society, and grant us his peace evermore, through Jesus Christ our Lord.

Lady Denning

MIDDLE TEMPLE

The grace used at the Middle Temple is an unusual version of the Fearon grace (Psalm 145 v. 15 and 16). There are conflicting theories about the origin and translation. Records at the Middle Temple indicate that it is a post-Reformation grace, adapted from Luther's '*Tischbot*' and printed in Day's black-letter Psalter, 1571. The grace has also been attributed to John Knox. To add to the confusion,

Cardinal Heenan referred to a pre-Reformation grace when he was made an Honorary Bencher in 1968.

Grace before Meat

The eyes of all things look up and put their trust in thee, O Lord: thou givest them their Meat in due season; thou openest thine hand, and fillest with thy blessing every living thing. Good Lord, bless us and these thy good gifts which we receive of thy bounteous liberality, through Jesus Christ our Lord. Amen.

Grace after Meat

Glory, honour, and praise be given to thee, O Lord, who doest feed us from our tender age, and givest sustenance to every living thing. Replenish our hearts with joy and gladness, that we, having sufficient, may be rich and plentiful in all good works, through Jesus Christ our Lord. God save his Church, the Queen, all the Royal Family, and this Realm: God send us peace and truth in Christ our Lord. Amen.

The Lord Salmon P.C.

A Judge's Grace, composed by the late Dr. R. R. Williams, Bishop of Leicester, for use in the Judges' Lodgings.

Gracious, O Lord, are thy gifts of food and drink;
Gracious, too, this place where we enjoy them.
Let gratitude fill our hearts with joy,
And equity the land with justice.
Through Jesus Christ our Lord. Amen.

A Grace for a Judges' Banquet at the Guildhall, composed by the Rev. Dr. B. A. C. Kirk-Duncan.

O God, who makest the sun to shine, on the just and
    on the unjust;
who givest food, to the thankful and the unthankful,
we would be numbered, amongst those, who ask thy
    blessing,
on this our meal, to be shared, one with another. Amen.

5

Societies and Organizations

Guide and Scout Graces. The graces from the Girl Guides dominate this section. According to the Chief Commissioner, the Guides sing graces at every opportunity, composing music for old words and making up words for old tunes. Most are set to music and many are sung as rounds. With their lyrical verses, expressing the joy of being alive, the Guide graces deserve to be more widely known. The Scouts do not have the same affinity to graces. There are no particular Scout graces and the choice is usually left to the boys or their leader.

A Three Part Round

Serve God Daily, taken from the sailing orders of *Sir John Hawkins*, 1532–95, a naval commander who fought the Spaniards and Portuguese for Elizabeth I. He sailed against the Spanish Armada in 1588 and was knighted after action off the Isle of Wight.

> Serve God daily, Love one another,
> Preserve your victuals, Beware of fire
> And keep good company.

> *A favourite grace of Mrs. Owen Walker,*
> *the Chief Commissioner,*
> *The Girl Guides Association*

Two Brownie Graces

> Hark to the chimes,
> Come bow your head,
> We thank thee, Lord,
> For this good bread.

Thank you for the hands that sow the grain,
Thank you for the hands that fish the sea.
Thank you for the sun-shine and the rain.
Thank you for the hands that care for me.

Two Guide Graces

Bless this our food,
And bless us in our Guiding
O Lord our God
To thee our praise shall rise.

Thank you for the meal before us spread,
For all those who worked to prepare it,
For the love that leads us to share it,
We thank you Lord, we thank you Lord.

God has created a new day

God has created a new day,
Silver and green and gold;
Live that the sunset may find us
Worthy his gifts to hold.

Ms. Joan Coleman

Rainy Day Grace

For dawn of grey and tattered sky,
for silver rain on grass and tree;
for song and laughter and work well done,
our thankful hearts we raise to thee.

A Four Part Round

Morning/Noontide/Evening is here,
The board is spread,
Thanks be to God,
Who gives us bread.

This Happy Meal

This happy meal will happier be
If we O Lord remember thee.

Mrs. Mabel E. Parham

Bees of Paradise. Words from an old Sussex rhyme.

Bees of Paradise
Do the work of Jesus Christ
Do the work that no man can.

A Blessing

If we have earned the right to eat this bread,
happy indeed are we;
But if unmerited thou givest to us,
may we more thankful be.

A Scout Grace by Bishop Brown. When Bishop of Birmingham, Bishop Laurence Brown made a habit of composing a different grace for almost every dinner he attended. He felt that a few arresting and sometimes irreverent words startled people into listening. This is just one example of his many graces. This grace was produced for the lunch given by the Lord Mayor to honour the Chief Scout, Sir

William Gladstone, when he was in Birmingham on January 19th, 1978, to attend the seventieth Anniversary of Birmingham Scouting. It was in fact a very wet and chilly day.

> We thank the Lord for fry-ups in the woods and on the
>   moors,
> We love the scent of wood-smoke, and the tang of
>   out-of-doors;
> But on this anniversary we offer up our praises
> That we're the Lord Mayor's honoured guests, not
>   lunching with the daisies.

Round Table. The National Association of Round Tables of Great Britain and Ireland have a grace which incorporates their maxim 'Adopt, Adapt and Improve'. The Bishop of Sodor and Man, the Rt. Rev. V. S. Nicholls, also gives this as his favourite grace.

> May we, O Lord, ADOPT thy creed,
> ADAPT our ways to serve thy need,
> And we, who on thy bounty feed,
> IMPROVE in thought, in word, and deed.

> *Denis Tizard*

Rotary

The Official Rotary Grace, with the emphasis on service before self.

> O Lord and Giver of all good,
> We thank thee for our daily food,
> May Rotary aims and Rotary ways
> Help us to serve thee all our days.

Another Rotary Grace

> We bless thee, Lord, for this our food.
> For life and health and every good.
> May we more blest than we deserve
> Live less for self and more to serve.

> *D. Cooke*

Inner Wheel. The Inner Wheel do not have an official grace, but many Clubs and Districts use the following grace. It originated in District 13, which covers the London area and was written for one of the District Chairmen during her term of office 1938/9.

> Father accept our thanks we pray
> For blessings showered on us each day
> And may thy love in friendship seal
> All members of the Inner Wheel.

> *Miss Jane Dobson*

Two Graces used by the Soroptimists—members of an international association of women's clubs.

> For food, for friendship
> And for the opportunity of Service,
> We thank thee, Lord.

> *Miss M. Mackie*

> For good food, good friends
> and good fellowship, we thank thee.

> *Miss N. A. E. Hibbert*

British Medical Association. A short simple grace was originally composed for the B.M.A. in 1966, but this did not meet with the approval of the many different religions within the Association. Various amendments were suggested and the present version bears little relationship to the original, being more of a prayer than a grace. However, it has the merit of approval from those representing some 75,000 doctors and incorporates the B.M.A. motto, 'With Head, Heart and Hand'.

The grace was first read out at a Chairman's lunch by the late Cardinal Heenan. As he sat down he said, 'I think that's good—you've got everything in it but the Manchester Guardian.'

> We thank thee, O Father, for our daily bread and all the blessings of this life: May thy blessed gift of healing so fill our lives that we serve our fellow men with head and heart and hand, and make the British Medical Association an instrument to that same end, to the honour and glory of thy name. Amen.

Sir Ronald Gibson

The Royal College of Surgeons of England. The College Grace was written by Rev. Adam Fox, Archdeacon of Westminster, at the request of the then President, Sir Harry Platt Bt., in 1957. The grace is used regularly at College dinners and has also been adopted by the Royal Australasian College of Surgeons.

> God grant grace to the Queen, wisdom and prosperity to this Royal College, and to every one of us a thankful heart for his good gifts today.

R. S. Johnson-Gilbert, O.B.E.

A Grace composed by Bishop Laurence Brown, when Bishop of Birmingham, for the British Hospitals Contributory Scheme Association National Conference Dinner, at Strathallan Hotel, Birmingham on October 7th, 1977.

> May God be praised, who taught us all
> That we should love our neighbours;
> And offer proof beyond fine words
> Resulting from our labours.
> So now we give our thanks to him,
> For one man's good example;
> And ask his blessing on the meal
> We're just about to sample. Amen.

W. G. Sherwood

The Pepys Club Grace. The grace is sung to Locke's 'Responses to the Ten Commandments', the same music which Pepys sang on Lord's Day, 1st September, 1667. The Rt. Rev. David Sheppard, Bishop of Liverpool, has a similar grace. (*Graces from The Bible*)

Bless the Lord, O my soul,
and forget not all his Benefits.
Who giveth food to all flesh,
for his mercy endureth for ever. Amen.

R. H. Adams

The Printers' Grace

For this food and through thy Holy Spirit,
The power to use aright the gift of tongues
And the printed word, we thank thee, Lord.

W. B. Morrell

The Miller's Grace

Back of the bread is the flour,
Back of the flour is the mill,
And back of the mill is the wind and the rain
And the Father's will.

Miss E. J. Allen-Williams

A Vegetarian's Grace

Lord, we thank thee for this our food, the fruits of the
earth of thy bountiful provision; and in our plenty
graciously incline our hearts and our thoughts in kindness and mercy towards thy creatures of the animal
kingdom over whom in thy wisdom thou hast en-
trusted us with dominion and stewardship.

A Grace suitable for Temperance Dinners!

Oh Jesus Christ,
Oh Lord Divine,
Who turnest the water into wine,
Pray forgive these foolish men
Who seek to turn it back again.

I. Bruce Lockhart,
Headmaster, Gresham's School

GRACES FROM THE WOMEN'S INSTITUTE

The original W.I. Grace from Canada

We thank thee, Father, for thy care,
Food, friends, and kindliness we share;
May we forever mindful be
Of Home and Country and of thee.

Mrs. A. E. Humphries

A Grace from the Queensland Country Women's Association, Australia

Great God, Creator of all, our heritage has been good,
we have not been short of the good things life has to
offer. May we always be thankful and express this by
our care of others, especially those who are less fortunate than we ourselves, through the C.W.A. and
similar 'helping hands' in our society. May our fellowship today be good and grow as we share this meal together. Amen.

Ms. Olive Blackmore

A Grace by Frances Turk, past County President and County Chairman for the Huntington and Peterborough Federation of Women's Institutes. Composed for the County Golden Jubilee celebrations in 1968.

> For the fruits of the countryside,
> the blessings of home and crafts,
> the spiritual ideals of truth,
> tolerance, justice and fellowship
> which we value and honour,
> may we be truly and lastingly thankful. Amen.

A W.I. Christmas Grace

> For holly's cheerful crimson berry,
> For children's faces shining merry,
> For all our loved ones gathered here,
> For absent loved ones far and near,
> For food to hearten us in eating,
> For wine to gladden us in drinking,
> For love, for health, for happiness,
> For joy and faith and hope of peace,
> For countless other gifts beside,
> We thank thee Lord this Christmastide.

Mrs. Bee Salsbury

The Stokenham (Devon) W.I. Graces

Grace before Dinner

> For the company we keep,
> and the food which we are about to partake,
> we thank thee Lord.

Grace after Dinner

Thank God for dirty dishes,
They have a tale to tell.
Whilst other folk go hungry
We've eaten very well.
For home, health, and happiness
We shouldn't make a fuss.
For by this pile of evidence,
God's been very good to us.

Mrs. Linda Archer

A Grace from the President of Shipley (Derbyshire) W.I.

Give us in all the trouble and sputter,
Our daily bread and a bit of butter.
Give us our health, our keep to make
And a bit to spare for others' sake.
Give us too a bit of a song,
And a tale and a book to help us along.
Give us Lord a chance to be
Our goodly selves, brave, wise and free,
Our goodly best, for ourselves and others
Till all men learn to live as brothers.

Ms. B. Loydall

The Grace said at Crick (Northampton) W.I. Golden Jubilee Dinner in 1975

> Lord, bless this food upon these dishes,
> As Thou didst bless the loaves and fishes.
> And like the sugar in the tea,
> May all of us be stirred by thee.

Miss Margery L. Collett

The Derwen (Clwyd) W.I. Grace, composed for their 21st Anniversary Dinner in 1970, by Mr. Arthur Roberts, a brother of one of the members.

Our Father who art in heaven.

We thank thee O Lord for being able to meet here this evening to celebrate our twenty-first Anniversary. We give thanks to thee for the countless blessings we have received each day over the years. We thank thee O Lord for the loyal service and happy memories of our dear members who have passed on to their rest. We hallow their memory still.

We pray for those members who cannot be with us tonight. O Lord we ask thee to bless our Homes and our Country. Help us O Lord to do what is right in thy sight. We ask for thy blessing on the food before us and on our meeting here tonight; for Jesus Christ's sake. Amen.

Mrs. E. C. Lewis

General Graces, to be used when a group of people meet informally together.

Heavenly Father, who has brought to our table such a variety of gifts from such a variety of sources to make one meal, grant that we be united together in one true fellowship of joy, through Jesus Christ our Lord. Amen.

R. Tudur Jones, Principal, Bala-Bangor College

Lord, as you shared food with your friends in Galilee, may this meal make us all grow in friendship. Amen.

Rt. Rev. M. Alexander, Bishop of Clifton

Bless, O Lord, our company,
our meal and those who have prepared it.
Through Christ our Lord. Amen.

Rt. Rev. Langton D. Fox,
Bishop of Menevia, North Wales

A Grace before parting

May God our Father bless this food, and this day,
that he may keep us safe in every way. Amen.

Rev. S. J. Riggs

6

Military & Maritime Graces

The maritime graces outnumber those from the other services in this section. Possibly there is more emphasis on formal dining on board ship and usually there is a chaplain on hand to say grace.

The shortest grace comes from the Navy, simply, *'Thank God!'* Sometimes this is prefaced by 'For what we are about to receive'.

Nelson's Grace, although Nelson, of course, said, 'God save the King.' This grace is frequently used by the Bishop of Salisbury, the Rt. Rev. G. E. Reindorp.

> God save the Queen,
> Bless our dinners;
> Make us thankful.

Other Graces from the Royal Navy

> God bless our Queen, our Dinner,
> and the Fleet in which we serve.
>
> *The Venerable B. A. O'Ferrall,*
> *Chaplain of the Fleet*

> Lord bless our meal,
> and the friendship of the table.
>
> *Rev. John Oliver,*
> *Chaplain of H.M. Naval Base,*
> *Portsmouth*

A Navigator's Grace

> Grant O Lord good fellowship to us who dine,
> Safety to all who cross the seas with us,
> Assurance to all who put their trust in us,
> through Jesus Christ our Lord.

> *Rev. Anthony M. Ross,*
> *Chaplain, Britannia Royal Naval College,*
> *Dartmouth*

The Honourable Company of Master Mariners' Grace, written especially for the Company by John Masefield in 1959.

John Masefield O.M. 1878–1967 and Poet Laureate from 1930. His lifelong interest in the sea is reflected in his poetry, with 'Dauber' and his 'Salt Water Ballads'. He was schooled for the merchant service and served his apprenticeship on a windjammer. Ill health drove him ashore and he then became a journalist and writer.

The Grace

> Let us give thanks for safety from the Sea,
> And for this bread with these our gathered friends.

Response to the Grace (to be said by all Hands)

> May the Light guide us till our sailing ends.

A Grace from the Merchant Navy, particularly relevant
during World War II.

> For what we are about to eat,
> Thank God and our Merchant Fleet.

> *Mrs. Kirsty Howat*

A Scottish Wartime Grace

> No ordinary meal—a sacrament awaits us
> On our tables daily spread,
> For men are risking lives on sea and land
> That we may dwell in safety and be fed.

A Grace by the Army Catering Corps

> For the food and drink we are about to receive,
> and for the skill of those who prepare and serve it,
> may the Lord make us truly thankful.

> *Rev. J. S. Cross*

The Soldiers' Grace

> You have walked with us in the valley
> You have stood with us on the hill.
> We ask only your Pity on the living
> And your Mercy on the dead.

> *J. Stanleigh Turner*

The Regimental Grace at the Royal Artillery Mess, Woolwich.

These words have been used in the Royal Regiment for many years and were also said at the Royal Military Academy, Woolwich, until it closed during the Second World War.

For what we are about to receive—Thank God.

> *Colonel R. H. Haynes, Royal Artillery Charitable Fund*

A Parachute Regiment Grace

> Good food,
> Good friends,
> Safe landings,
> Thank God.

> *Mrs. Yvonne Ellis*

An anonymous contributor sent the following 'grace'. A bishop who was unexpectedly taken into an officers' mess and asked to say grace, is said to have blurted out, *'God bless this Mess'* before he could collect his wits!

A Grace composed by Cecil Hunt and used when Chairman of the Paternosters Club, during the Battle of Britain.

> For good fellowship in freedom
> and for those who made it possible,
> we give thanks.

A Grace from the Royal Air Force. The R.A.F. do not have any formal graces and the chaplain is usually asked to say a grace of his own choice. However, this grace, composed by Group Captain E. F. Haylock, R.A.F. (Retd.), has been commended to all R.A.F. chaplains by the Chaplain-in-Chief, R.A.F.

For the spirit of adventure which takes us into the air,
For God's grace which brings us safely back to earth,
For the comradeship which draws us together,
For the blessing of good food,
For these and all his mercies God's holy name be praised.
Amen.

R. Widdup

7

Regional Graces

Traditional Scottish Grace

O Lord, who blessed the loaves and fishes,
Look doon upon these twa bit dishes,
And though the taties be but sma',
Lord, make 'em plenty for us a';
But if our stomachs they do fill,
'Twill be another miracle.

A Grace from the East coast of Scotland

Gracious Peter look o'er the table
Eat na' mair na ye are able
When ye're done, lay by yer spoon,
Gracious Peter. Amen.

Mrs. D. Thornhill

Old Galloway Grace

Bless the sheep for Davit's sake,
   he herdit sheep himsel';
Bless the fish for Peter's sake,
   he gruppit fish himsel';
Bless the swine for Satan's sake,
   he was aince a swine himsel'.

Miss Sarah Jackson

An old Scottish Grace

Stick in till you stick oot.

M. B. Mavor, Headmaster, Gordonstoun School

Perthshire Children's Grace

Doon head
Up paws
Thank God
We've jaws. Amen.

Ms. A. Methuen

A Light-hearted Grace

Scones and pancakes roun' the table,
   Eat as much as ye are able,
Eat a'! Pooch nane!*
   Hallelujah! Amen.

Mrs. Montgomery

*Leave nothing.

Gaelic 'Rune of Hospitality'

I saw a stranger yestreen;
I put food in the eating place,
Drink in the drinking place;
Music in the listening place;
And, in the sacred name of the Triune,
He blessed myself and my house,
My cattle and my dear ones.
And the lark said in her song,
Often, often, often,
Goes the Christ in the stranger's guise;
Often, often, often,
Goes the Christ in the stranger's guise.

*Sir Ian Macdonald of Sleat, Bt., who
adds that the 'Rune of Hospitality' was
given to his great-grandmother in 1914
by Nurse Ross.*

A Grace in Gaelic by Iain MacCodrum, the Uist bard.

The people had gathered to release water from Loch Hastin and celebrated with a dram. The person in charge asked Iain to say grace. He sniffed his glass and said: —

> Gum beannaicheadh dia uisge Loch Hàsdain
> Ma 's math 'àileadh 's fheàrr a bhlas
> Is ma tha e mar seo gu léir
> Bu mhór am beud a leigeil as.

> God bless the water of Loch Hastin.
> If its smell is good, better is its taste.
> And if it is all like this,
> What a pity to let it go!

Rev. Roderick Macdonald

An Anecdote about a Grace in Gaelic

The following interchange took place in Dingwall, when the famous Baptist preacher, Spurgeon (1834–92), went North to open the new church for Dr. Kennedy. An Elder had said the grace in Gaelic and Spurgeon asked after the blessing, 'What language was that?' 'Oh,' said Dr. Kennedy 'do you not know, it was the language of our first parents in the Garden of Eden.' 'Ah,' said Spurgeon, 'no wonder they were put out!'

Dr. G. K. Mackenzie

Robert Burns 1759–96, wrote several of our best-known graces. The Selkirk Grace is said by Scots all over the world on Burns Night, 25th January.

The Selkirk Grace. The poet having been on a visit to the Earl of Selkirk at St. Mary's Isle, was asked to say grace at dinner. He repeated the following words, which have since been known as The Selkirk Grace.

1 Some hae meat, and canna eat
   And some wad eat that want it;
   But we hae meat and we can eat,
   And sae the Lord be thankit.

A Grace before Dinner—a favourite grace of the Baroness Pike, Chairman W.R.V.S.

2 O thou, who kindly dost provide
   For every creatures want!
   We bless thee, God of nature wide,
   For all thy goodness lent;
   And, if it please thee, heavenly Guide,
   May never worse be sent;
   But whether granted or denied,
   Lord, bless us with content! Amen.

A Grace on a Sheep's Head. Having been dining at the Globe Tavern, Dumfries, on one occasion when a sheep's head happened to be the fare provided, Burns was asked to give something new as a grace, and instantly replied:—

3 O Lord, when hunger pinches sore,
   Do thou stand us in stead,
   And send us from thy bounteous store
   A tup or wether head! Amen.

After having dined, and greatly enjoyed this dainty, he was asked again to return thanks, when, without a moment's premeditation, he at once said:—

> O Lord, since we have feasted thus,
> Which we do so little merit,
> Let Meg now take away the flesh,
> And Jock bring in the spirit! Amen.

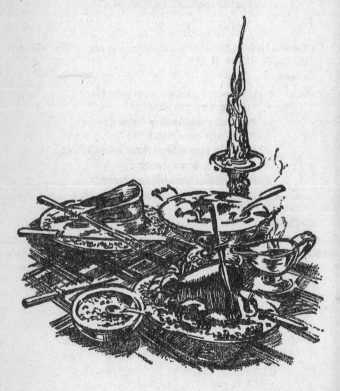

Graces used at one time by six of the seven Incorporated Trades of Aberdeen. These Trade or Craft Guilds date back to the fifteenth century. At one time they were influential in protecting their members' interests, but they now exist for educational and charitable purposes.

Hammermen

1   Our art over all, mechanics hath renown
Our arms, the hammer and the royal crown.

Bakers

2   May he the sun of righteousness display
On all our actions his celestial ray
May we in peace our daily bread possess
And smiling providence our labour bless
Contented may we live and die resigned
And in the skies a crown or glory find.

Fleshers

3   Whilst we do sheep and oxen slay
Frail mankind here to feed
Help's Lord to pray our father this day
Give us our daily bread.

Shoemakers

4   As we make shoes for others' feet
Lord grant we may be shoed
With gospel peace which is most meet
While here we make abode.

Weavers

5 As the weavers' shuttle palseth in place
   So help us Lord to spend our days in grace
   That so our hearts may still united be
   To Jesus Christ and all eternity.

Wrights and Coopers

6 Our trades is renowned by sea and land
   By timber work completed by our hand
   Which trades practised by us are holden rare
   As witness our compass, adze, and square.

Curlers' Grace

THANKS BE TO GOD, for he doth send
The ample board, the honest friend—
The social joys of wit and mirth
All good companionship on earth.

THANKS BE TO HIM for seasons' round
For Spring's first touch on barren ground,
For Summer's prodigal display,
For Autumn's bitter-sweet decay.

THANKS BE TO GOD for that strong hand
Protecting now the sleeping land,
When all is held in Winter's vice
Thanks for the *glory of the ice*.

*Rt. Rev. G. K. B. Henderson, M.B.E.,
Bishop of Argyll and The Isles*

Dean Ramsay's Blessing. During the eighteenth century, Bishops and members of the Episcopal Church in Scotland were subject to the Penal Laws. Congregations were forbidden to meet and so church people met in their own homes in groups of four to five and the Bishops travelled around to minister to the faithful. In a book of recollections of traditions in Scottish life, published in 1874, Dean Ramsay recalled that it was customary for the Bishops to say the following Blessing or Grace.

> God Almighty bless thee with his Holy Spirit,
> Guard thee in thy going out and coming in,
> Keep thee ever in his faith and fear,
> Free from sin, and safe from danger.

> *Rt. Rev. Frederick Goldie,*
> *Bishop of Glasgow and Galloway*

IRELAND

An Irish Blessing or Grace, before parting.

> May the road rise to meet you,
> May the wind be always at your back,
> May the sun shine warm on your face,
> The rain fall softly on your fields.
> And until we meet again
> May God hold you in the palm of his hand.

A Grace from the Sixth Century. This is a grace used on formal occasions and has a special ring about it, characteristic of Irish Celtic Christianity.

> May the blessing of the loaves and fishes
> which our Lord shared among the multitude,
> and grace from the King who made the sharing,
> be upon us and our partaking.

> *The Most Rev. George O. Simms,*
> *Archbishop of Armagh*

Graces in Irish Gaelic

Altú roimh Béile Grace before Meals

> Beirimid buíochas do Dhia as ucht an bhia seo atáimid ag dul a chaitheamh tré Chríost ár dTiarna. Amen.

> We give thanks to God for this food which we are about to eat, through Christ, Our Lord. Amen.

Altú tar éis Béile Grace after Meals

> Glacamid buíochas do Dhia as ucht an bhia seo atáimid tar éis a chaitheamh tré Chríost ár dTiarna. Amen.

> We give thanks to God for this food which we have eaten, through Christ, Our Lord. Amen.

> *Dr. Séamas Ó Catháin, University College, Dublin*

Graces by Bishop Thomas Wilson, Bishop of Sodor and Man, from 1697–1755, from his book *Sacra Privata*.

Grace before Meat

> O God, who givest food unto all flesh, grant that we may receive these thy Gifts with thy Blessing, and use them with sobriety and thankfulness, through Jesus Christ our Lord. Amen.

Grace after Meat

> May God, who hath given us bodily food, give us also spiritual food, and life, through Jesus Christ our Lord. Amen.

Graces in Manx Gaelic

Unfortunately, no original graces have been written in Manx Gaelic, but the following are used.

> Booise da Jee er son nyn mee.

> Thanks to God for our food.

> Coon-jee les ny h-annoonee my vees oo lajer
> Cur graih da'n chenndiaght my vees oo aeg
> S'lhiat y foill my t'ou aggairagh
> Cum dty hengey my vees oo corree.

Help the weak if you are strong
Love the old if you are young
Own the fault if you are wrong
Hold your tongue if you are angry.

Mrs. Audrey Ainsworth,
Secretary of the Manx Gaelic Society

WALES

The englyn by W. D. Williams, Barmouth, is one of the most widely used graces in schools and homes throughout Wales today.

O Dad, yn deulu dedwydd—y deuwn,
A diolch o'r newydd,
Can's o'th law y daw bob dydd
Ein lluniaeth a'n llawenydd.

O Father, a contented family—we come
With renewed thankfulness,
Because from thy hand there comes each day,
Our sustenance and our happiness.

A Grace by Rev. Pennar Davies, Principal, Memorial College, Swansea, for all Christian gatherings.

Roddwr pob rhoddiad daionus a phob rhodd berffaith, bendithia dy bobl, yma ac ymhob man, wrth dderbyn, wrth roi ac wrth rannu. Trwy'r Croeshoeliedig, Amen.

Giver of every good and perfect gift, bless thy people here and everywhere, in their receiving, their giving and their sharing. Through the Crucified, Amen.

The Amman Valley Comprehensive School Grace, Ammanford, Dyfed (the old Amman Valley Grammar School). The grace is no longer said at the school.

> Diolchwn i Ti am holl roddion dy ragluniaeth,
> yn enw ein Harglwydd Iesu Grist. Amen.

> We thank thee for all the gifts of thy providence, in the name of Our Lord, Jesus Christ. Amen.

D. Eirwyn Morgan, Principal, North Wales Baptist College,
Bangor

A Grace from Coleg Bala-Bangor

> Bendithia dy roddion hyn, a sancteiddia ni yn ein mwynhad ohonynt, a maddau ein beiau, yn Iesu Grist ein Harglwydd. Amen.

> Bless these thy gifts, and sanctify us as we enjoy them, and forgive us our sins, through Jesus Christ our Lord. Amen.

R. Tudur Jones, Principal, Coleg Bala-Bangor

A Grace used by the 101 year old mother of the Bishop of Swansea and Brecon.

> Am iechyd da a bwyd bob pryd
> Moliannwn di O Dduw.

> For good health and every meal
> We praise thee O God.

Rt. Rev. B. N. Y. Vaughan,
Bishop of Swansea and Brecon

Nonconformist Graces from '*Rhodd Mam*' by the late John Parry, Chester.

O Arglwdd, bendithia'n bwyd, i'n cadw'n fyw i'th wasanaethu Di, drwy Iesu Grist. Amen.

O Lord, bless our food, to keep us alive to serve thee, through Jesus Christ. Amen.

Diolch i ti, O Arglwydd, am ein bwyd, ac am bob trugaredd. Dyro ras i ni i fyw yn dduwiol wrth eu mwynhau, er mwyn Iesu Grist. Amen.

Thank thee O Lord, for our food and for every mercy. Give us grace to live godly lives while enjoying them, for Jesus Christ's sake. Amen.

Mrs. E. Edmunds

A Grace in both English and Welsh

I Dad y trugareddau i gyd boed clod a moliant, parch a bri,

To the father of all mercies let there be praise and glory, reverence and fame,

Followed by, Bless O Lord these thy gifts to our use and ourselves to thy service, for Jesus Christ's sake.

Rt. Rev. E. M. Roberts, Bishop of St. Davids

The graces collected from the English regions, tend to be rather irreverent and humorous, with a good sprinkling from Yorkshire.

> Meat for t'belly
> t'belly for t'meat;
> God gave both—praise the Lord.
> Let battle commence, Albert.

The Rt. Rev. H. V. Whitsey, Bishop of Chester, heard this grace many years ago in a Yorkshire farmhouse. The farmer sat at the head of the table, with his eldest son, Albert, at his right hand—both were poised with a knife and fork in their hands.

An Old Yorkshire Grace

> Thank the Lord for
> waat we've getton.
> If ther'd been any moor
> it wud a been etton.

Mrs. M. Tyas

Another Grace from Yorkshire

> Thank God for this bit—
> Some folk would have made a meal of it.

Mrs. N. M. Barugh

A Yorkshire Grace, reported from the old 'Craven Hiefer' Inn, Skipton, where huge Yorkshire teas were served. There is a similar grace in a West Country dialect.

Grace before Meat

May t'Lord mak us able to eat whats ont table.

Grace after Meat

Now, t'Lord be praised our stomacs be aised.

The authoress, Miss Dorothy Hartley

A Grace from a Scilly Island fisherman

The Lord be praised,
My belly's raised
An inch above the table;
And I'll be damned
If I'm not crammed
As full as I am able!

Mrs. K. Middleton

The Wessex Prayer

God bless me and me wife,
Me son John and his wife,
    Us four:
    No more!

8

Graces round the World

Seigneur, bénissez notre nourriture et ceux qui
l'ont préparée, qu'elle fortifie nos corps et
notre amitié. Dieu, notre père, donnez-nous
la joie de vous aimer comme des frères, en
mangeant le même pain. Amen.

Lord, bless our food and those who have
prepared it, so that it strengthens our bodies and
our friendship. God, our father, give us
the joy of loving you like brothers,
by eating the same bread.

Mon Dieu, bénissez ce repas,
et procurez du pain a ceux qui
n'en ont pas.

My God, bless this meal,
and give food to those who
have none.

Mrs. Pauline Rae

A Family Grace, usually sung as a round.

Pour ce repas,
Pour toute joie
Nous te louons, Seigneur.

For this meal,
For every joy
We praise you, Lord.

Rt. Rev. P. C. Rodger,
Bishop of Oxford

A Children's Grace

> Bien mangé,
> Bien bu,
> Merci, petit Jesu.

> I've had plenty to eat,
> I've had plenty to drink,
> Thank you little Jesus.

> *E. V. Morgan, Headmaster,*
> *Sacred Heart School,*
> *Tunbridge Wells*

SWITZERLAND

Switzerland is half Catholic and half Protestant and has a variety of graces, some in German and others in French.

A Grace by the French Poet, Clément Marot, 1496–1544, a Protestant, whose graceful and witty style influenced many contemporary and later writers.

> Père éternel, qui nous ordonnes
> N'avoir souci du lendemain,
> Des biens que pour ce jour nous donnes
> Te mercions de cœur humain.
> Or puisqu'il t'a plu, de ta main,
> Donner au corps manger et boire,
> Plaise-toi du céleste pain
> Paître nos âmes, à ta gloire. Amen.

Eternal Father, who commands us not to take thought for the morrow, we give thee thanks from human hearts for the things which thou givest us for this day. Now since it hath pleased thee, with thy hand, to give food and drink for the body, may it please thee to feed our souls with the heavenly bread, for thy glory. Amen.

Minister of the Eglise Suisse de Londres

One of the most common graces in the German speaking parts of Switzerland is the German grace, 'Komm Herr Jesus . . .' (see page 87).

A Prayer used by both Protestants and Catholics alike. Graces usually rhyme and in the last twenty years it has become common to make up a prayer on the spot, often with a humorous note to make people smile.

Für Trocken und Nass – Deo Gratias!

For dry and wet – thanks be to God!

Rev. Father Paul Bossard

A Grace in Swiss Dialect. The following grace was heard from an old Swiss who probably made it up himself. It is in Swiss dialect—a language which is seldom written (some say maliciously, a language to curse in, but not to pray!).

Liäbe Gott, lass üs bim ässe
Dyni Güeti nid vergässe!

Dear God, while we eat our food,
Let us not forget that you are good!

Rev. Father Paul Bossard

An Old German Grace before Meat, which is one of the most widely used graces in Germany today and is similar to a grace attributed to Luther.

>Komm, Herr Jesus, sei unser Gast
>und segne, was du uns bescheret hast.

>Come, Lord Jesus, be our guest
>and bless what thou hast given us.

>*Rector Felix Leushacke*

A Popular Grace after a Meal

>Danket dem Herrn, denn er ist sehr freundlich
>und seine Güte währet ewiglich.

>Thanks be to the Lord for he is bountiful
>and his mercy endureth forever.

>*Pastor Helmut Tacke*

A Family Grace

>Gott, lass uns alle,
>die wir um diesen Tisch versammelt sind,
>einander lieben.

>Oh God, let us all
>gathered here at this table,
>love one another.

>*Pastor Helmut Tacke*

Other Graces before Meals

Wir danken dir, Herr Jesu Christ,
dass du unser Gast gewesen bist.
Bleib du bei uns, so hat's nicht not.
Du bist das wahre Lebensbrot.

We thank thee, Lord Jesu Christ,
That thou art our guest.
Remain with us so that we may not suffer want.
Thou art the true bread of life.

Pastor Helmut Tacke

Du gibest Speise reichlich und überall,
nach Vaters Weise sättigst du allzumal;
du schaffest früh'n und späten Regen,
füllest uns alle mit deinem Segen.

Thou givest food in abundance
and like a father thou satisfiest us at all times;
Thou providest rain early and late
and fillest us with all thy bounty.

Pastor Helmut Tacke

Gott, wir danken,
dass wir zusammen essen dürfen.
Sei auch bei denen,
die beim Essen allein sind,

Oh God, we thank thee
that we are able to eat together.
Be thou also with those who eat alone.

Pastor Helmut Tacke

Roman Catholic families in Holland usually say the Lord's Prayer, followed by Ave Maria. In the past, Protestant families used to ask for a blessing before the meal and thank God afterwards. Nowadays, most people just say a short grace before a meal.

Two Children's Graces

Heer, zegen deze spijze. Amen.

Lord, bless this food. Amen.

Heer, heb dank
voor spijs en drank. Amen.

Lord, (we give) thanks
for what we eat and drink. Amen.

A Family Grace, which can be sung and often people hold hands to form a circle around the table.

Voor alle goede gaven, Heer,
zij U de dank en eer. Amen.

For all good gifts, Lord,
thanks and honour be to you. Amen.

Older people in Holland still sing a moralistic prayer, reflecting former Calvinistic soberness. The following grace was composed by Hendrik Ghysen, who died in 1693. Significantly, it has been omitted from the latest edition of the hymnbook.

Grace before Meals

O Vader, die al 't leven voedt,
kroon onze tafel met uw zegen,
en spijs en drenk ons met dit goed,
van uwe milde hand verkregen!
Leer ons voor overdaad ons wachten,
dat w'ons gedragen als 't behoort;
doe ons het hemelse betrachten,
sterk onze zielen door uw Woord!

O Father, who feeds all that lives,
crown our table with thy blessings
and feed and water us with these good things
that we get from thy generous hands!
Teach us to refrain from excesses,
that we may behave as is proper;
make us exercise the heavenly things,
strengthen our souls with thy Word.

Grace after Meals

O Heer, wij danken U van harte
voor nooddruft en voor overvloed;
daar menig mens eet brood der smarte,
hebt Gij ons mild en wel gevoed.
Doch geef, dat onze ziele niet
aan dit verganklijk leven kleve,
maar alles doe wat Gij gebiedt,
en eindlijk eeuwig bij U leve!

O Lord, we thank thee from our hearts
for what we needed and what was extra;
so many people eat bread with sorrow,
but you have nourished us generously and well.
Yet give that our soul will not

cling to this transitory life,
but do all that you command
and in the end will live with you for ever!

Information on Dutch graces by Rev. J. J. Vogel,
the Dutch Church, London

NORWAY

A Traditional Table Grace

Before the Meal

> I Jesu navn går vi til bords,
> å spise, drikke på ditt Ord.
> Deg Gud til ære, oss til gavn,
> så får vi mat i Jesu navn. Amen.

> In Jesus' name we go to the table,
> to eat and drink according to your word.
> To God's glory and to our benefit
> we receive our food in Jesus' name. Amen.

After the Meal

> For mat og drikke du oss gav,
> for din velsignelse derav,
> for daglig brød fra faderhånd,
> lær oss å takke ved din ånd.

> For food and drink you gave us,
> your blessing from these gifts,
> for daily bread from fatherly hand,
> teach us to give thanks through your spirit.

A Table Grace for children, which can be sung as a round

O du som metter liten fugl,
velsign vår mat o Gud.

O you who feeds the little bird,
bless our food, O Lord.

A Modern Norwegian Grace, translated from the Swedish

Gledens Herre vær vår gjest ved vårt bord i dag.
Gjør vårt måltid til en fest etter ditt behag.

The Lord of joy, be our guest at our table today.
Make our meal a celebration according to your will.

Norwegian graces contributed by Pastor Dagfinn Kvale,
Norwegian Seamen's Church, London

SWEDEN

A Traditional Swedish Grace

I Jesu namn till bords vi gå,
Välsigna Gud, den mat vi få.
Oss alla av det brödet giv
Som giver världen evigt liv.

In Jesu's name we gather here,
Bless, Lord, our food and be us near.
Give us, we pray, that bread divine
Which grants us ever to be thine.

Sven Evander, Rector,
The Swedish Church, London

DENMARK

Velsign vort hus, velsign vort bord,
velsign den hele vide jord,
og lær os med taknemmelig ånd
at tage alting af din hånd.

Bless our house, bless our table,
bless the whole wide world,
and teach us to take everything
gratefully from Thy hand.

Din miskundhed, Herre, os mætter,
giv os et taknemmeligt sind,
og giv, at vi daglig fletter
dit navn i vor gerning ind.

Your mercy, O Lord, satisfies us,
give us a grateful mind as well,
and grant that daily we weave
your name into our work.

Rev. Poul-Erik Fabricius,
the Danish Vicar in London

A Popular Finnish Grace

> Siunaa Jeesus ruokamme,
> ole aina luonamme.
>
> Jesus bless our food,
> and be always with us.

Markku Tapio, Pastor,
Finnish Seamen's Mission,
London

RUSSIA

Russian Orthodox Church

Grace before Meals

The eyes of all creatures are turned towards thee, O God, with hope, and thou givest them their meat in due season; thou openest thy hand and they are all filled with good things.

Grace after Meals

We thank thee, O Christ our God, that thou hast satisfied us in thy bounty; deprive us not of thy heavenly Kingdom, but as thou didst come to thy disciples and granted them thy Peace, come also to us and save us.

Metropolitan Anthony of Sourozh

Russian Orthodox Church Outside Russia

Grace before the Evening Meal

The poor shall eat and be filled, and they that seek the Lord shall praise him; their hearts shall live for ever, and ever. Glory to the Father, and to the Son, and to the Holy Spirit, both now and ever, and unto the ages of ages. Amen.

Lord have mercy (Thrice).

Christ God, bless the food and drink of thy servants, for thou art holy, always now and ever, and unto the ages of ages. Amen.

Fr. Alexis, The Russian Orthodox Church in Exile

GREECE

Greek Orthodox Church

Save, O Lord, thy people and bless thine inheritance. Accept our thanks for these thy creatures, given to us for our sustenance, and keep us under thy protection and guidance, through Christ our Lord. Amen.

The late His Eminence Archbishop Athenagoras,
Greek Orthodox Archdiocese of Thyateira and Great Britain

TURKEY

A Grace to be said at the end of a Family Dinner.

May God increase our/your prosperity.

Vahap Asiroglu, Turkish Embassy, London

CYPRUS

The Bishop in Cyprus and The Gulf, the Rt. Rev. L. J. Ashton, uses a simple grace, which is particularly useful when members of other faiths are present.

For these and all his mercies, thanks be to God. Amen.

IRAN

An Iranian Grace, in farsi script, which the children enjoy singing.

Bar-ā-yeh attā-yā-yeh bee had-deh-tow,
Ku-nam bā del oh jon hammee hamd-deh tow.

For unnumbered blessings and all gifts of thine,
Our heartfelt thanksgiving to thee we assign.

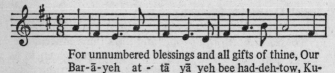

For unnumbered blessings and all gifts of thine, Our
Bar-ā-yeh at - tā yā yeh bee had-deh-tow, Ku-

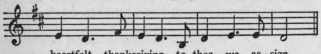

heartfelt thanksgiving to thee we as - sign.
nam bā del oh jon hammee hamd-deh tow.

Rt. Rev. H. B. Dehqani-Tafti, Bishop in Iran, who narrowly escaped an assassination attempt in 1979

EGYPT

The Coptic Orthodox people make the sign of the Cross and then say the Lord's Prayer in Arabic. Others say:—

Lord we give you thanks for this food,
remember the poor and needy.

or

O Lord who fed the multitudes with five barley loaves,
bless what we are about to eat. Amen.

Rt. Rev. Ishaq Musaad, Bishop in Egypt with North Africa,
Ethiopia and Somalia

FROM AN AFRICAN DIALECT

The Bread is pure and fresh,
The Water cool and clear
Lord of all life, be with us
Lord of all life, be near.

Rev. J. B. Gower

KENYA

**A Grace composed by the Most Rev. Dr. F. H. Olang',
The Archbishop of Kenya.**

O, Lord God, our Father in heaven, who has called us and has given us new life in Christ, the Saviour of mankind, we continue to praise your holy name for the fellowship we have with each other. We pray for abundant blessing upon these gifts of food for our use in his dear name. Amen.

TANZANIA

A Grace in Swahili, used by Anglican Christians.

Before Eating

Mwenyezi Mungu utubariki, ukibariki na chakula hiki unachtupa, ili tukikitumia tupate nguvu za kukutumikia vema. Amen.

Bless us, O Almighty God, and bless this food which you are giving us, that it may give us strength to serve you well. Amen.

After Eating

Mwenyezi Mungu tunakushukuru sana kwa chakula hiki ulichotupa, na kwa baraka zako zote. Amen.

We thank you, O Almighty God, for this food which you have given us, and for all your blessings. Amen.

The Most Rev. John Sepeku, Archbishop of Tanzania

ZIMBABWE

A Shona Grace, with a refreshing literal translation.

Before Meals

Komborerayi Tenzi zwipo iswi tiri Kugashira kubva mumanja enyu Imi Jeso Kristo Tenzi Wedu. Amen.

Bless the Lord these gifts we are receiving from thy heavenly blessings, Lord Jesus Christ. Amen.

After Meals

Baba tatenda nekudya kwamatipa pane anomanheru,
Kuburikidza nezita ratewzi wedu Jesu Kriste. Amen.

We thank you Lord for the meal you have offered us
this evening. Through the Name of our Lord Jesus
Christ. Amen.

CENTRAL AFRICA

**A Grace from Chilema United Church Lay Training
Centre,** which is jointly owned by Anglicans, Catholics,
Presbyterians and Churches of Christ. The grace was for-
mulated out of a need to have something simple in which all
the lay trainees could participate at meal times.

Lord,
With hearts full of happiness,
And thankful for the food before us,
We thank you, Lord, for the food,
For your gifts which you give us every day,
And for life which will last forever, Amen.

*The Most Reverend Donald Arden,
Archbishop of Central Africa*

A Prayer composed by Archbishop Trevor Huddleston and used regularly as a grace before meals at Bishopscourt when Archbishop Joost de Blank was Archbishop of Cape Town.

> God bless Africa,
> Guide her rulers,
> Guard her peoples,
> And give her peace,
> Through Jesus Christ our Lord. Amen.

The Rt. Hon. David Steel, M.P., Leader of the Liberal Party, who adds that at a time when the question of human rights is attracting an ever increasing attention, it is perhaps fitting that we should remember the example of these two great men, who devoted their lives to the cause of the oppressed peoples of South Africa.

U.S.A.

President Jimmy Carter's White House Grace

> God is great, God is good,
> Let us thank him for our food.

A Grace used by President Eisenhower. A similar grace was reported by Ms. Doris Wood, who was taught the grace when she lived in Bolton, Lancs, over sixty years ago.

> Lord Jesus be our Holy guest,
> Our morning prayer
> Our evening rest,
> And with this daily food impart
> Thy love and grace to every heart.

> *Miss Letitia Smith, Ontario,*
> *Canada*

A Grace used by the early Pioneers in America, 1840–50, which shows a proper respect for their own labours, as well as an appreciation for the Lord's bounty.

Lord, we work mighty hard for these here vittles, but we thank you jes' the same. A-men.

The broadcaster, Irene Thomas

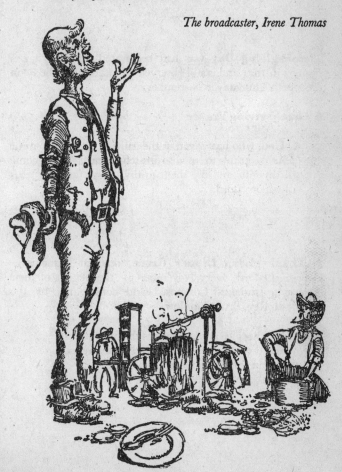

An early Californian Grace

> Good food,
> Good meat,
> Good God,
> Let's eat.

> *G. Leutzinger*

Thanksgiving Day was first celebrated by the Pilgrim Fathers in 1621 and is still observed as a national holiday on the fourth Thursday in November.

A Thanksgiving Prayer

> O God, who hast given us the fruits of the earth for our delight, grant to us also grateful hearts to welcome all thy gifts and use them to thy glory, through Jesus Christ our Lord.

> *Mrs. Sybil Harton*

A Thanksgiving Dinner Grace, used at Manchester College, Oxford, every November for the benefit of their American students. Composed and contributed by the Principal, Rev. Bruce Findlow.

> For the faith and courage of the first harvest
> and the first thanksgiving and for many more,
> for our families and friends far and near,
> thanks be to God. Amen.

A Grace after Meat from the Holy Cross Monastery, West Park, New York.

The King of eternal Glory make us partakers of his heavenly table. Amen.

Rev. Canon J. Macquarrie,
Lady Margaret Professor of Divinity, Oxford

A Family Grace

As we partake of earthly food,
At this table thou has spread,
We'll not forget to thank thee, Lord
For all our daily bread. Amen.

Mrs. Winifred Hewitt,
who heard this grace every day when she
visited her sister in America

Graces from *We Gather Together*: A Cookbook of Recipes by the Wives of the Bishops of the Episcopal Church.

Set our hearts at liberty from the service of ourselves and let it be our meat and drink to do thy will.

Dear Lord we thank thee for this food—may it nourish our souls and bodies. As we gather together as a family we ask thy blessing on our love for each other.

Mrs. Sybil Harton

For food and friends and all God sends,
We praise his holy name.

Miss E. J. Allen-Williams

A Grace from the Most Rev. E. W. Scott, Primate of Canada

O God, our father,
In a world where many are lonely we thank you for friendship and community;
In a world where many are despairing, we thank you for hope;
In a world that many find meaningless, we thank you for faith;
In a world where many are hungry we thank you for this food.
Through Christ, our Lord. Amen.

9

Different Religions

Hebrew Proverb

He who eats and drinks, but does not bless the Lord, is a thief.

An Ancient Hebrew Prayer, dating back to the age of the Pharisees and probably Jesus.

Blessed be thou Lord God of the universe
who bringest forth bread from the earth
and makest glad the heart of men.

*A grace frequently used by the Most Rev. and
Rt. Hon. Stuart Blanch, Archbishop of York*

A Modern Jewish Grace before Meals

For the food we are about to eat,
and for all that sustains us,
we give thanks to the Creator
and Sustainer of life.

*Dr. Louise Davies,
Head of the Geriatric Nutrition Unit,
Queen Elizabeth College,
University of London*

Grace after Meals

Blessed art thou, O Lord our God, King of the universe, who feedest the whole world with thy goodness, with grace, with lovingkindness and tender mercy; thou givest food to all creatures, for thy lovingkindness endureth for ever. Through thy great goodness food hath never failed us: O may it not fail us for ever and ever for thy great name's sake, since thou nourishest and sustainest all beings, and doest good unto all, and providest food for all thy creatures whom thou hast created. Blessed art thou, O Lord, who givest food unto all.

Moshe Davis, Office of the Chief Rabbi

Other Graces of Jewish Origin

Blessed be he, Lord God of the Universe,
by whose goodness we live and by whose bounty we eat.

Rt. Rev. S. W. Phipps, Bishop of Lincoln

Blessing and honour and power and might
be unto our God for ever and ever.

Rt. Rev. J. M. Bickersteth,
Bishop of Bath and Wells

Blessed be God, King of the Universe, who has created all things living, and hast supplied the means to sustain the life of each of them—Blessed is he, the life of all the world.

Rev. J. B. Gower

A Hindu Grace

Whatever I eat is of God, and from God,
and is mine as I am his.

Rev. J. B. Gower

A Grace in Sanskrit, which is part of the prayers in Candi
or Devisátaka, eleventh or twelfth century. It is a very popular religious text in Bengal, and is connected with the annual
September festival (Pūjā).

Yā devī sarvabhūtesu ksudhārūpena samsthitā namastasyai
namastasyai namastasyai namo namah.

I bow down to that Goddess who lives within everybody in the form of Hunger.

Professor B. K. Matilal,
Professor of Eastern Religion and Ethics, Oxford

A Prayer from China

Each time we eat
May we remember God's love.

Japan. The grace originates from Buddhism. Originally the grace was said to Buddha, but today it is said to the parents or the person who cooks the meal.

Grace before Meals

Itadakimasu.

Thank you for the meal.

Grace after Meals

Gochisosama

Thank you for a lovely meal.

Akiko Shindo, Japanese Information Centre, London

The concept of 'grace', as such, is rare in Buddhism and each school of Buddhism varies in its use of set prayers before meals. The following prayers are from the Japanese Soto Zen tradition, as set out in *Selling Water by the River* by the Rev. Jiyu Kennett, and English *roshi* or Zen master, at present Abbess and Spiritual Director of Shasta Abbey, U.S.A.

From the Vimalakìrti Sūtra*

When one is identified with the food one eats, one is
identified with the whole universe; when we are one
with the whole universe, we are one with the food we
eat.

* Scripture or discourse

The following prayers are recited at breakfast. In this
country they are used at Throssel Hole Priory, Hexham,
Northumberland.

This prayer is said whilst the food is being served

We will first share the merits of this food with the
Three Treasures of the Dharma,*
Second, we will share it with the four benefactors,
the Buddha, the President/Queen, our parents and all
    people;
Third, we will share it with the six lokas;*
With all of these we share it and to all we make offering
    thereof.
The first bite is to discard all evil;
The second bite is so that we may train in perfection;
The third bite is to help all beings;
We pray that all may be enlightened.
We must think deeply of the ways and means by which this
    food has come.
We must consider our merit when accepting it.
We must protect ourselves from error by excluding greed
    from our minds.
We will eat lest we become lean and die.
We will accept this food so that we may become enlightened.

* Dharma—the teachings of the Buddha.
* lokas—the six worlds (heaven, the world of humans, the

world of dissension, the world of animals, the world of hungry ghosts, hell).

Recited when everyone has finished eating

We offer this water to the spirits of the departed so that they too may be filled.

Graces or Prayers said before meals, from the book *Muslim Prayers*

DU'A At the time of beginning a meal

In the name of ALLAH and with the blessings of ALLAH

DU'A After a meal

Praise be to ALLAH, who gave us food and drink and made us Muslims.

DU'A When dining at the table of another person

O ALLAH! Bless them in that which You have provided for them and forgive them and have mercy upon them.

Dr. M. A. Zaki Badawi, Director, The Islamic Cultural Centre

A Prayer from the East

I pray the Prayer the Easterns do
May the Peace of Allah abide with you.
Wherever you stay or wherever you go
May the beautiful Palms of Allah grow.
In your days of labour and nights of rest

May the Peace of Allah still keep you blest.
And I touch my heart as the Easterns do
May the Peace of Allah abide with you.

J. Stanleigh Turner, who has used this prayer as
a grace. He does not know its origin, but believes
that it is ascribed to W. J. Nathams

10

Graces from Christian Churches

A Prayer at Dinner-time from the Apostolic Constitution

> Thou art blessed, O Lord, who
> nourishest me from my youth,
> Who givest food to all flesh.
> Fill our hearts with joy and gladness,
> That at all times having all sufficiency,
> We may abound to every good work
> in Christ Jesus our Lord;
> With whom to thee be glory, honour and might,
> For ever and ever. Amen.

A Grace from the Leonine Sacramentary, attributed to Leo the Great, Pope 440–461. The manuscript dates from the seventh century.

> May the sacred feast of thy table, O Lord, always strengthen and renew us, guide and protect our weakness amid the storms of the world, and bring us into the haven of everlasting salvation, through Jesus Christ our Lord.

Graces taken from the Sacramentary of Saint Gelasius, Pope 492–496, another early liturgical manuscript, dating from the seventh or eighth century.

Prayers before Food

> Refresh us, O Lord, with thy gifts, and sustain us with the bounty of thy riches, through Jesus Christ our Lord.

> May thy gifts, O Lord, be our refreshment, and thy grace our consolation, through our Lord.

Prayer after Food

Satisfied, O Lord, with the gifts of thy riches, we give
thee thanks for these things which we receive from thy
bounty; beseeching thy mercy that that which was
needful for our bodies may not be burdensome to our
minds, through Jesus Christ our Lord.

The traditional Roman Catholic grace is a translation of a
Latin prayer, from the Gelasian Sacramentary, chanted in
monastic or religious communities.

Grace before Meat

Bless us O Lord and these thy gifts, which we are about
to receive from thy bounty, through Christ our Lord.
Amen.

Grace after Meat

We give thee thanks, Almighty God, for all thy benefits, who livest and reigneth world without end. (May
the souls of the faithful departed, through the mercy of
God, rest in peace.) Amen.

A Variation from the Bishop of Leeds

Bless us O Lord and these your gifts which we are about
to receive of your kindness, And keep us mindful of
those in want. Amen.

Rt. Rev. W. G. Wheeler, Bishop of Leeds

A Grace from the Bishop of Clifton

Lord as we share the food that you give us, help us to share all your gifts.

Rt. Rev. M. A. Alexander, Bishop of Clifton

Two Graces from St. Francis' Prayer Book

Give us grace, O Lord, to be ever thankful for thy providence, with hearts always ready to provide for the needs of others.

Blessed Lord, we pray thee
To be present at our table,
Hallowing thy gifts to our use;
That eating to satisfy our needs
We may remember those who lack.

A Grace from the Roman usage

Edent pauperes, et saturabuntur:
et laudabunt Dominum qui requirunt eum.
Vivent corda eorum in saeculum saeculi.

The poor shall eat, and have their fill,
and those who seek the Lord shall praise him.
They shall live in joy for ever and ever.

Followed by

Benedic Domine nos, et haec tua dona,
quae de tua largitate sumus sumpturi.

Bless us, O Lord, and these thy gifts,
which we are about to receive from thy bounty.

A Medieval Grace

> Largitor omnium bonorum
> benedicat cibum et potum servorum suorum.

> May the giver of all good things
> bless the food and drink of his servants.

Rev. Dr. John McHugh, University of Durham

The Doxology is often sung as a grace. This is taken from Morning and Evening Hymns by Bishop Ken, 1637–1711 and is the last verse in the Hymns 'Awake my Soul' and 'Glory to Thee', which are usually sung to the tune 'Old Hundredth'.

> Praise God from whom all blessings flow,
> Praise him, all creatures here below,
> Praise him above, angelic host,
> Praise Father, Son and Holy Ghost.

The Traditional Anglican Grace is derived from a similar grace in *The Christian's Daily Devotion*, S.P.C.K. 1769 and is probably the most widely used grace today.

> Bless O Lord this food to our use
> and us to thy service,
> and make us ever mindful of the needs of others. Amen.

A Variation from the Most Rev. Trevor Huddleston, Archbishop of Mauritius.

> Bless O Lord this food to our use,
> supply the need of others and give us thankful hearts.

A Grace by Bishop John Dowden, 1840–1910, Bishop of Edinburgh from 1886 and a scholar of the medieval and early Celtic Church in Scotland.

O Lord Jesus Christ, who hast taught us that man does not live by bread alone, feed us, we humbly beseech thee, with the true bread that cometh down from Heaven, even thyself O Blessed Saviour, who livest and reignest, with the Father and the Holy Spirit, one God, world without end.

The Archbishop of Canterbury, the Most Rev. Robert Runcie, composed this grace on his way to a banquet in London, when Bishop of St. Albans.

For food and drink and friendship, we render thanks. Bless, O Lord, our table; deepen our gratitude; enlarge our sympathies and order our affections in generous and unselfish lives, for Jesus Christ's sake. Amen.

The Rt. Rev. David Brown, Bishop of Guildford, frequently uses this grace at public functions, varying the second and fourth lines to suit the occasion.

God save the Queen:
God guard our (College/County/etc.)
God bless this food;
God keep us all;
through Jesus Christ, our Lord. Amen.

The Rt. Rev. E. A. J. Mercer, Bishop of Exeter, has a similar grace.

> God save the Queen:
> God keep the Realm:
> God prosper our fellowship:
> God bless our food
> And give us thankful hearts.

A Grace from the Bishop of Winchester the Rt. Rev. J. V. Taylor

Be present at our table, Lord, for in the breaking of our bread we remember thee.

A Grace used by the Bishop of Norwich the Rt. Rev. M. A. P. Wood

Almighty God, our Heavenly Father,
You give to us summer and winter, seedtime and harvest,
and the assurance of food and providence
and Fatherly care.

Accept our thanks for this meal;
meet the needs of those who are facing the
insecurities of life today;
and grant to us—in our fellowship tonight—
one more provision—
the gift of a thankful heart,
through Jesus Christ our Lord.

Rev. M. N. W. Burch, the Bishop of Norwich's Lay Chaplain

A Grace by the Rt. Rev. J. Poole-Hughes, Bishop of Llandaff, especially composed for this collection.

> Grant, Lord, your blessing on our meat that all the strength from what we eat may serve your holy Will. Grant that our sharing in this meal may make more true the love we feel for you and for our friends. Grant that our pleasure may remind us of the needs of all mankind for food and knowing you. Amen.

The Archbishop of Papua New Guinea and Bishop of Port Moresby, the Most Reverend G. D. Hand, has a variation of the offertory prayer used in many modern Christian Eucharistic Liturgies.

> Blessed are you, Lord, God of all creation.
> Through your goodness we have this food to eat
> And this fellowship to enjoy.
> Bless the food for our use.
> Bless us in your service,
> And help us to help those who are in need,
> For Jesus Christ's sake. Amen.

One of the best known Nonconformist graces was written in 1741 by the Moravian writer, John Cennick 1718–55, an evangelist who worked with the Wesleys in the West Country and Ireland before joining the Moravian Church. Both the graces, before and after meat, were painted on a gallon-size teapot which Josiah Wedgwood made for John Wesley.

The graces were published in *Sacred Hymns for the Children of God in the Days of Their Pilgrimage* in 1741. The grace before meat has been translated into Welsh and Cornish.

Grace before Meat

> Be present at our Table, Lord,
> Be here and everywhere ador'd:
> These creatures bless and grant that we
> May feast in Paradise with thee.

The Salvation Army sometimes change the last line to:

1. May spend our lives in serving thee.
2. May live to fight and die for thee.
3. May meet in Paradise with thee.

Grace before Meat — in Welsh

Bydd wrth ein bwrdd O Frenin Ne'
Boed iti fawredd ym mhob lle,
Bendithia 'nawr ein hymborth ni
A gad in' wledda gyda thi. Amen.

Mrs. E. Edmunds

And Cornish

Byth omma, arluth dh'agan prys;
Gordhyes re by dres oll an bys
Son agan bos, ha gront dhyn ny
Yn nef bos megysgenes sy.

John W. Gittins

J. Cennick's Grace after Meat

We bless thee, Lord, for this our food,
But more for Jesus' Flesh and Blood,
The manna to our spirits given,
The living Bread sent down from Heaven.
Praise shall our grateful lips employ:
While life and plenty we enjoy.
Till worthy, we adore thy Name,
While banqueting with Christ the Lamb.

A Grace written by Cennick's son-in-law, John Swertner, 1746–1813.

> Lord, the gifts thou dost bestow
> Can refresh and cheer us too;
> But no gift can to the heart
> Be what thou, our Saviour, art.

Two Graces by James Montgomery, poet and hymn-writer 1771–1854. The verses from one of his Communion hymns are sometimes used as graces, with the last verse referring to the story of the Emmaus Road.

> We would not live by bread alone,
> But by that word of grace,
> In strength of which we travel on
> To our abiding place.

> Be known to us in breaking bread,
> But do not then depart;
> Saviour, abide with us, and spread
> Thy table in our heart.

A Grace from another Montgomery hymn

> O bless the Lord my soul,
> His mercies bear in mind,
> Forget not all his benefits;
> the Lord to thee is kind.

> *Rev. Fred. Linyard,*
> *the Moravian Church*

There are many Wesleyan Graces. John Wesley, 1703–91, is said to have taught the duty of saying grace and Charles Wesley, 1707–88, assisted by publishing special tracts.

Two Graces by Charles Wesley 1746

Lord of all, thy creatures see
Waiting for their food on thee;
That we may with thanks receive,
Give, herewith thy blessing give.
Fill our mouths with food and praise,
Taste we in the gifts the Grace,
Take it as through Jesus given
Eat on earth the Bread of Heaven.

Blessing to God, for ever blest,
To God the Master of the feast,
Who hath for us a table spread,
And with his daily bounties fed;
May he with all his gifts impart
The crown of all—a thankful heart.

Two Graces by Dr. W. W. Kay, Past President of Independent Methodist Churches and Moderator of the Free Church Federal Council. Both graces can be sung.

We thank thee, Lord, for this our food,
And for thy loving ways;
In all things always thou art good;
To thee be all our praise.

Bread of life come down from heaven,
Grace and mercy freely given,
Feed us from thy boundless store,
Daily, Lord, and evermore.

John M. Day, General Secretary,
Independent Methodist Churches

Two Graces by Rita Snowden, a deaconess of the New Zealand Methodist Church.

1   God receive our thanks for the gifts of many seasons, and the service of many hands. Amen.

2   O God, ever generous in the nourishment of our bodies, nourish our spirits too, we pray. Amen.

May God relieve the wants of others and give us thankful hearts; for Christ's sake.

Rev. Dr. Kenneth G. Greet, Secretary of the Methodist Conference

For food, for friends and for the Hope of Glory,
We give you thanks, O Lord.

Rev. Charles G. Eyre, Secretary of the Conference,
the Methodist Church in Ireland

The Grace used by General Arnold Brown, Salvation Army, who adds that the graces used by Salvationists are often extempore or composed for a particular occasion. Many of the graces are sung.

O God, our Heavenly Father: Once again thy beneficent hand has provided for the needs of our body, and as we partake of this food, may we also, in abundant measure, partake of that divine grace which alone can nourish the soul. This we pray in the Name of Jesus our Lord. Amen.

Charles Haddon Spurgeon, 1834–92, the celebrated Baptist preacher, wrote this short grace in 1866.

> We thank thee Father, for the love
> Which feeds us here below
> And hope in fairer realms above
> Celestial feasts to know.

For all thy gifts, dear Lord, and all thy goodness, we are truly grateful: bless them to our use—and keep us in thy faith and fear, for Jesus' sake.

Rev. R. E. O. White, Principal, Baptist Theological College
Scotland

Graces from a Baptist Cook Book, produced by the Home Mission Fund Working Group in 1977.

For all good things, thanks be to God.

Great is thy goodness, grace, mercy and bounty,
And for all these things we bless thy name.

Rev. David S. Russell, General Secretary
of the Baptist Union of Great Britain and Ireland

A Grace by the Rt. Rev. Alfred Martin, a former Moderator of the Presbyterian Church in Ireland.

O Great Provider, grant us grace to show our gratitude for this food, by being mindful of thy servants who prepared it for our enjoyment, even as Jesus Christ would have us be. Amen.

Rev. Robert R. Cox

Do thou bless our meal today, and may thy Spiritual Presence fill us with gratitude for all these abundant blessings. Amen.

We give thee thanks, for life and all its blessings. Give thou this food to nourish our bodies, and thy Word of Truth to sustain our souls. Amen.

The Rt. Rev. John R. Gray,
Moderator of the General Assembly of the Church of Scotland

Graces used at the Unitarian College, Manchester

For food and fellowship, for all good gifts, we thank thee Lord.

For these and all other mercies, God's Holy Name be praised.

Rev. A. J. Long, Principal, Unitarian College, Manchester

Gerald Priestland, the B.B.C.'s religious affairs' correspondent is a Quaker and although he does not normally use a spoken grace, he has composed a grace for this collection. Traditionally, Quakers do not 'say' grace, but stand in silent meditation before the meal.

As we assemble round the board
We do as did our Heavenly Lord.
And for his Church our Lord Divine
Chose fellowship and bread and wine.

Lord Mancroft's mother was a Quaker and taught him the old, plain Quaker grace. He finds it particularly useful when the company is of all colours, races and creeds.

Us and this; God bless.

II

Religious Communities

Two Graces from the Convent of the Holy Name, Malvern Link, Worcestershire.

> Lord, as we live by thy bounty
> may we live to thy glory.

The refrain from the German hymn, *'We plough the fields and scatter'*, by Matthias Claudius, 1740–1815, as a grace.

> All good gifts around us
> Are sent from heaven above;
> Then thank the Lord, O thank the Lord,
> For all his love.

The Fearon Grace, 'The eyes of all wait upon Thee, O Lord . . .', from Psalm 145, v. 15 and 16, is the most widely used grace in Anglican religious communities. It originates from the monastic office or form of service, when the grace was in Latin and much longer than today, consisting of a psalm, the Kyrie, the Lord's Prayer, Collect and a lesson. Here are two adaptations of the Fearon grace.

Grace used at the Society of Saint John the Evangelist, Oxford.

V. The eyes of all wait upon thee, O Lord.
R. And thou givest them their meat in due season.
V. Thou openest thine hand.
R. And fillest all things living with plenteousness.
V. Glory be to the Father and to the Son and to the Holy Ghost.
R. As it was in the beginning, is now and ever shall be. Bless, O Lord, these gifts to our use, and us to thy service. Amen.

At the end of the meal

    V.   All thy works praise thee, O Lord.
    R.   And thy saints give thanks unto thee.
    V.   They show the glory of thy kingdom.
    R.   And tell of thy power.
    V. and R. The Gloria.
        We thank thee, O God, for these and all thy gifts,
        through Christ our Lord. Amen.

Grace from Tyburn Convent, Hyde Park Place, London,
an enclosed order in the centre of London.

Grace before the Meal

    V.   The eyes of all creatures
    R.   look to you, O Lord, and you give them their
        food in due time. You open wide your hand,
        grant the desires of all who live. Praise the Father,
        the Son and the Holy Spirit, for ever and ever.

        Let us pray: Bless us, Lord, bless us and these
        your gifts which we receive from your bounty.
        Through Christ our Lord. Amen.

Grace after the Meal

    V.   All your creatures
    R.   shall thank you O Lord, and your friends shall
        repeat their blessing. Praise the Father, the Son
        and Holy Spirit, for ever and ever.

Let us pray: We give you thanks, almighty God, for
all your gifts. Through Christ our Lord. Amen.

The Grace from the Benedictine Community of Nashdom Abbey, Burnham, Bucks. The grace was composed by the Community in 1971 and has subsequently been adapted and adopted by other religious communities. As in the Jewish tradition, the stress is upon 'Blessed be God', rather than upon the specific blessing of the food.

Grace before Meals

V.   In the name of the Father, and of the Son, and of the Holy Spirit.

R.   Amen.

V.   Blessed be God, the Creator of all things.

R.   Thanks be to Him who has given us life and all that sustains it.

V.   Let us pray for all those through whom our food is provided.

R.   Bless them, O Lord.

Reader: Whether you eat or drink, or whatever you do, do all to the glory of God.

R.   Amen.

Grace after Meals

Reader: Lord, have mercy upon us.

R.   Thanks be to God.

V.   Let us who have shared in this meal pray for each other.

R.   May God unite us in heart in His service.

V.   Let us pray for all who are in hunger and need.

R.   Bless them, O Lord.

V.   May the Lord who has fed us on earth bring us to share His banquet in heaven.

Graces from the Society of Saint Francis, Hilfield
Friary, Dorchester.

Two Graces regularly used in the refectory

Lord we thank you for this nourishment to feed our
bodies: we ask you to nourish our hearts in faith and
love; that we may praise you as you richly bless us:
through Jesus Christ our Lord.

Lord you have brought us to this place to share a life
of Christian brotherhood: give us a thankful heart for
all your mercies, and bless our meal and fellowship
together: through Jesus Christ our Lord.

A Grace from the Community of the Sacred Passion,
The Convent, East Hanningfield, Essex.

May this that I take refresh me, and thy Passion
strengthen me. Lord Jesus I thank You.

Just one example of a grace from a Roman Catholic community is given, the **Loreto Sisters, Institute of the
Blessed Virgin Mary,** Dublin. As in the old monastic
tradition, they have many different graces and prayers,
some for ordinary time and others for feast days and litur-
gical seasons.

V.   The Lord is close to all who call him, who call on
     him in their hearts.
R.   We will bless your Name for ever, O Lord.

Before Dinner

May we take this meal with gladness of heart, O Lord, rejoicing that we belong to you and to each other. We make our prayer through Christ our Lord.

R.   Amen.

After Dinner

Father, through this meal you have renewed us in the spirit of love and unity. Help us to bear constant witness to your love and to make our community a living gift to others. We make our prayer through Christ our Lord.

R.   Amen.

De Profundis—Psalm 29 or 129.

12

Graces with the Hungry in mind

A Grace by Bishop Charles Gore, 1853–1932, Bishop of Worcester, Birmingham and then Oxford. With his strong personality and controversial views, he is said to have exercised an unequalled influence on the Church during his lifetime.

Lord, forgive us that we feast while others starve.

Gwyn Thomas, the writer and novelist from Wales, gives his own formula of gratitude at a feast and remembers the less fortunate.

Let us be thankful for whatever light, laughter, food and affection may come our way. And let us be mindful equally of those who at this or some future moment may be sadly without any or all of these good and golden things.

Delia Smith, the cookery writer and television presenter, comments that one third of the world's population suffers from the effects of over-eating whilst the other two thirds live at or below subsistence level. With this in mind, she offers the following grace.

We thank and praise you Lord for the gifts of your creation and ask your blessing on mankind that one day we can learn to share with poorer nations so that no-one will go hungry. We ask you this through Jesus Christ our Lord. Amen.

A Girl Guide World Hunger Grace, used by the Hunger Task Force Anglican Church, Diocese of Huron, Canada.

> For food in a world where—
> many walk in hunger;
> For faith—in a world where—
> many walk in fear;—
> For friends in a world where—
> many walk alone,
> We give you humble thanks O Lord.

A Grace after Meat, from Manchester College, Oxford.

In a somewhere hungry, sometimes lonely world, for this food and this fellowship may we be truly thankful. Amen.

Rev. Bruce Findlow, Principal

A Grace from Bala-Bangor College

Merciful Father, whose will it is that none of thy children should suffer want, grant that we, as we enjoy these thy gifts, may be ever mindful of those who are in need, through Jesus Christ, our Lord.

R. Tudur Jones, Principal

Rev. Dr. John McHugh, University of Durham, has written a grace for Nottingham University students, 'for those particularly interested in food and drink'.

We praise thee, O God, who bringest forth food from the earth, and wine that makes glad the heart of man.

And we humbly beg thee, Lord, to look down from heaven upon the souls that are hungry, and to fill them with all good things.

> Let us remember the hungry,
> and thank God for our food.

A. C. S. Gimson, M.B.E., Headmaster, Blundell's School,
Devon, who uses this grace daily in his own home

The Roman Catholic Archbishop of Liverpool, the Most Rev. Derek Worlock, has said the following grace for the last fourteen years. He adds that it is good to remember those who have helped to make the meal and to remind people who attend public functions, that in many parts of the world one course might represent a full diet for a week.

> Bless us, O Lord, and bless this food.
> Bless those who have prepared it,
> and bless all the hungry people in the world. Amen.

A Grace from the Bishop of Chester, the Rt. Rev. H. V. Whitsey, who added the second part to the Anglican grace some years ago, when he used to take a number of boys from a large 'overspill' housing estate to the Isle of Man for a camp each summer. This grace was said at every meal in order to awaken their minds to the people in the world who still did not get regular food.

> Bless, O Lord, this food to our use and us
> to thy service
> and provide for the wants of others less
> fortunate than ourselves,
> for Jesus Christ's sake. Amen.

A Grace from the Rev. Richard B. R. Walker, expressing its message with simplicity.

> May God be praised and thanked
> for all his bounty,
> and keep us mindful of those in need.

A Grace by the Rev. J. B. Gower

> Lord, grant us grateful hearts, we pray,
> For all our needs supplied this day;
> With food sufficient, may we plead,
> Mind aware of others' need.

A Grace by Rita Snowden, a deaconess of the New Zealand Methodist Church.

> In this hungry world, we truly pray—
> O God, we bow before this meal,
> mindful of the needs of others,
> thankful you meet our own.

Perhaps it is fitting to conclude this chapter with a grace from the **Director-General of OXFAM.** As a Quaker, **Mr. Brian Walker** says a silent grace before meals in his own home.

> A silent grace, sometimes holding hands, family and guests alike, in which we thank God for our food, our health and fellowship as a family, and remember that each day 90,000 members of the human family die from starvation or malnutrition, whilst a further 25,000 die from thirst or water-borne diseases.

13

Schools & Colleges

Schools. In the popular imagination, the older established schools have their own traditional graces. Unfortunately, this is no longer the case. With the introduction of cafeteria style catering in so many schools, the graces have lapsed. At Aldenham School, Elstree, Herts, for example, their sixteenth-century Latin grace remembering their founder, Richard Platt, was discontinued in 1974, when the school changed to central catering. Some schools retain long Latin graces for formal occasions, but with the easing out of Latin from the school curriculum, it is questionable how much longer these will be used.

Some schools use variations of the Fearon Grace (Graces from the Bible) or the traditional Anglican grace, 'Bless O Lord this food to our use . . .' or, the Roman Catholic grace, 'Bless us O Lord and these thy gifts . . .', others have their own individual graces. The choice of grace is often left to the discretion of the Headmaster/mistress and the most widely used public school grace is still the simple Latin grace, as at **Ellesmere College, Shropshire.**

Grace before Meat

Benedictus Benedicat per Jesum Christum Dominum Nostrum.

Let the blessed bless, through Jesus Christ our Lord.

Grace after Meat

Benedicto Benedicatur per Jesum Christum Dominum Nostrum.

Let the blessed be blessed through Jesus Christ our Lord.

D. J. Skipper, Headmaster, Ellesmere College

Winchester College, founded in 1382, by William of Wykeham, Bishop of Winchester. The Winchester College grace dates back to the seventeenth century. For the first two centuries, the grace was sung, not recited, but in 1867 there were complaints about the quality of the singing and the grace was then spoken. Until 1900, the grace was sung occasionally on Sundays.

Today the grace is said before lunch each day by the Prefect of the Hall. Before the first part, he says 'Surgite', to get all the scholars on to their feet.

Grace before the Meal

Benedic nobis, Domine Deus, atque eis donis tuis quae de tua largitate sumus sumpturi, per Iesum Christum Dominum nostrum.

Bless us, Lord God, and these thy gifts which of thy bounty we are about to receive, through Jesus Christ our Lord.

Grace after the Meal

Agimus tibi gratias, omnipotens Deus, pro his et universis donis tuis quae de tua largitate accepimus, qui vivis et regnas et es Deus in saecula saeculorum.

We give thee thanks, almighty God, for these and all thy gifts which of thy bounty we have received, who liveth and reigneth and art God for ever and ever.

The Warden and Fellows of Winchester College

Christ's Hospital, Horsham, Sussex, founded in London, in 1553 by King Edward VI. Both graces were written by Bishop Henry Compton 1632–1713, Bishop of Oxford and then London. He supported William of Orange and crowned William and Mary in 1689.

Grace before Meat

Give us thankful hearts, O Lord God, for the Table which thou hast spread for us. Bless thy good creatures to our use, and us to thy service, for Jesus Christ his sake. Amen.

Grace after Meat

Blessed Lord, we yield thee hearty praise and thanksgiving for our Founder and Benefactors, by whose Charitable Benevolence thou hast refreshed our bodies at this time. So season and refresh our Souls with thy Heavenly Spirit that we may live to thy Honour and Glory. Protect thy Church, the Queen, and all the Royal Family. And preserve us in peace and truth through Christ our Saviour. Amen.

P. J. Attenborough, Headmaster, Sedbergh School

The Reading Blue Coat School, founded in 1646 by Richard Aldworth, a merchant of London and Reading.

Before Breakfast

May the Lord bless this food for our use and us in his service, and help us to remember the needs of others, for Christ's sake. Amen.

After Breakfast

Thou hast given so much to us; give us one thing more, a grateful heart, for Christ's sake. Amen.

Before Lunch

Blessed Lord, may the food which we are about to receive strengthen our bodies, and may thy Holy Spirit strengthen and refreshen our souls, for Christ's sake. Amen.

After Lunch—as at Christ's Hospital, Horsham. (See page 144.)

Before Tea

May God relieve the wants of others and give us thankful hearts, for Christ's sake. Amen.

After Tea

For these and for all thy gifts we give thee thanks. Amen.

C. P. Nobes, Headmaster, Bedales School

King William's College, Isle of Man, endowed in 1668.

Grace before Meat

> Benedic Domine nobis et his donis Tuis, quae de Tua gratia et munificentia sumus iam sumpturi, et concede ut, illis salubriter a Te nutriti, Tibi debitum obsequium praestare valeamus, per Iesum Christum Dominum nostrum. Amen.

> Bless us, O Lord and these thy gifts, which from thy grace and generosity we are now about to consume, and grant that, healthily nourished with them by thee, we may be strong to furnish to thee due obedience, through Jesus Christ our Lord. Amen.

Grace after Meat

> Pro bono cibo et sodalitate bona, Te Deum laudamus; necessitates quoque aliorum obsecramus sustine, ut Tibi semper gratias agamus, per Iesum Christum Dominum nostrum. Amen.

> For good food and good companionship we praise thee God. Supply also, we beg, the needs of others, so that we may always give thee thanks, through Jesus Christ our Lord. Amen.

P. K. Bregazzi, Principal, King William's College

The Grace used by the Children of the Foundling Hospital, Guildford Street, London. The school was founded in 1739 by the philanthropist Captain Thomas Coram, for the care of destitute children. Many children were dead on arrival and records show that between 1756 and 1760, 15,000 children were admitted to the Hospital, of whom only 4,400 lived. The school had many famous patrons, including Hogarth, Handel, Thackeray and Dickens. The Hospital moved from Guildford Street in 1926 and now exists as a charity for unmarried mothers.

Father of Mercies, by whose Love abounding
All we thy Creatures are sustained and fed;
May we while here on Earth thy praises sounding
Up to thy Heavenly Courts in joy be led.

St. Ninian's School, Moffat, Dumfriesshire. This boys' preparatory school was founded a hundred years ago and the grace probably dates from that time. As far as is known, the grace is unique to the school, and is not said elsewhere. The Latin words are used.

Before Meals—from Psalm 136, v. 1.

V.   Confitemini Domino quoniam bonus:
R.   Quoniam in aeternum eius misericordia. Amen.

V.   We confess to the Lord because he is good:
R.   Because his mercy is everlasting. Amen.

After Meals—from Psalm 68 v. 19.

   V.   Benedictus Dominus die quotidie:
   R.   Prosperum iter faciet nobis Deus salutarium
        nostrorum. Amen.

   V.   Blessed be the Lord today and everyday:
   R.   The Lord will make a happy journey of our good
        fortune. Amen.

P. G. Spencer, Headmaster, St. Ninian's School

Colleges. Most of the Oxford and Cambridge Colleges
have their own individual graces. Many of these are derived
from the old monastic forms and often they have been
shortened to suit modern needs. The long graces that have
been retained are usually only used for formal occasions.
As this book is aimed at the general reader, only a few
examples of Latin graces are given.

King's College, Cambridge, founded 1441.

Benedic, Domine, nobis, et his donis tuis, quae tua
gratia et munificentia sumus iam sumpturi; et concede
ut illis salubriter a te nutriti tibi debitum obsequium
praestare valeamus per Christum Dominum nostrum.
Amen.

Lord, bless us and these thy gifts which with thy grace
and bounty we are now to eat; and grant that, nourished
therewith by thee to our health, we may honour thee
with the praise which we owe thee, through Christ our
Lord. Amen.

Lord Annan

Christ's College, Cambridge, founded in 1505.

Grace before Meals. The grace used before meals is one of several dating from the foundation of the College and has been in use continuously since that time. It may well have been composed by Bishop Fisher of Rochester, 1459–1535, the Lady Margaret's Chaplain and Confessor, who was a friend of Erasmus and More. He was beheaded in 1535 for refusing to acknowledge King Henry VIII as the supreme head of the Church.

> Exhilarator omnium Christe, sine quo nihil suave, nihil jucundum est; benedic, quaesumus, cibo et potui servorum tuorum, quae iam ad alimoniam corporis apparavisti; et concede, ut istis muneribus tuis ad laudem tuam utamur, gratisque animis fruamur; utque quemadmodum corpus nostrum cibis corporalibus fovetur; ita mens nostra spirituali verbi tui nutrimento pascatur, per Te Dominum nostrum.

> Christ the gladdener of all, without whom nothing is sweet or pleasant, bless, we beg you, the food and drink of your servants, which you have now provided for our bodily sustenance; and grant that we may use these gifts to praise you, and may enjoy them with grateful hearts; grant too that, just as our body is nurtured by bodily foods, so too our mind may feed on the spiritual nourishment of your word, through you our Lord.

Translation by Dr. D. N. Sedley.

Pembroke College, Oxford, founded in 1624. When Dr. Samuel Johnson visited St. Andrews University in 1773, he was surprised to learn that a 'scholarly' university like St. Andrews did not have a full Latin grace. He then quoted the Pembroke College grace after meat, by the historian Camden, 1551–1623. According to Boswell, Dr. Johnson could still repeat his old College grace towards the end of his life.

The grace by Camden is seldom heard now at Pembroke College and is only said on formal occasions. Over the years, leave was given to the lower tables to withdraw before the high table had finished dinner, so a grace before meat was introduced in 1887. Today, this grace is read by a Scholar in the Hall every night. At the end of dinner, the Master usually says 'Benedicto Benedicatur'.

Grace before Meat

Pro hoc cibo quem ad alimonium corporis nostri sanctificatum es largitus, nos Tibi, Pater omnipotens, reverenter gratias agimus; simul obsecrantes ut cibum angelorum, panem verum coelestem, Dei Verbum aeternum Jesum Christum Dominum nostrum nobis impertiare, ut Eo mens nostra pascatur, et per carnem et sanguinem Ejus alamur, foveamur, corroboremur. Amen.

For this food which thou hast bestowed on us and hallowed for the nourishment of our body we give thee reverent thanks, Almighty Father, beseeching thee also that thou wilt let us partake of the food of Angels, the true bread of Heaven, the everlasting Word of God, Jesus Christ our Lord, that our mind may feed on him and that through his Body and Blood we may be nurtured, cherished and strengthened. Amen.

Camden's Grace after Meat, as quoted by Dr. Johnson.

Gratias Tibi agimus, Deus Misericors, pro acceptis a Tua bonitate alimentis; enixe comprecantes ut serenissimum nostrum Regem (Georgium), totam regiam familiam, populumque Tuum universum tuta in pace semper custodias. Amen.

We give thee thanks, merciful Lord, for the nurture we
have received by thy goodness; beseeching thee ear-
nestly that thou will keep safe our most serene High-
ness, (King George), all the royal family and thy whole
people, and ever guard them in thy peace.

G. Arthur, Master, Pembroke College

University of St. Andrews, founded in 1411. As a result
of Dr. Johnson's comments about the lack of a Latin grace
at St. Andrews, the Professor of Humanity was asked to
write a grace. Unfortunately, this was so long that the
President could only give one sentence from memory, 'Sit
nomen domini benedictum' followed by 'Deo gratias' at the
end of the meal. These words were used as the grace at the
University until Sir A. C. Mackenzie wrote the words and
music for another blessing and grace in 1896. This runs as
follows and is still in use today.

Blessing

Sit nomen Domini benedictum per Jesum Christum
salvatorem nostrum. Amen.

Blessed be the name of the Lord, through Jesus Christ
our Saviour. Amen.

Grace

Gloria Patri Filio spirituique sancto in saecula saeculorum. Amen.

Glory to the Father, the Son and the Holy Ghost for
ever and ever. Amen.

R. N. Smart, Keeper of the Muniments,
University of St. Andrews — Manuscript 139

Christ Church, Oxford, founded in 1546.

Grace before Meat. This is the first half of the full grace before meat and these words have been used at Christ Church for the past three hundred years.

> Nos miseri homines et egeni, pro cibis quos nobis ad corporis subsidium benigne es largitus, Tibi Deus omnipotens, Pater coelestis, gratias reverenter agimus; simul obsecrantes, ut iis sobrie, modeste atque grate utamur, per Jesum Christum Dominum nostrum.

> We, poor and needy men, reverently give thee thanks, Almighty God, Heavenly Father for the food which thou hast bestowed on us for the sustenance of the body, at the same time beseeching that we may use them soberly, modestly and gratefully, through Jesus Christ our Lord.

David Dimbleby

King's College, London, founded in 1829.

The Grace before Dinner was said in the College Halls of Residence until late 1974 when, at the instigation of the students, it was discontinued.

> God be praised for all his mercies. God preserve the Church, the Queen and King's College, and grant his grace for evermore.

I. M. Howard

Some Theological College Graces

Mansfield College, Oxford. Mansfield College has the distinction of having a grace translated from Welsh into Latin and then into English. The original was composed in Welsh by Sir Ifor Williams for Neuadd Reichel, University College of North Wales, Bangor. As a compromise to the English students who objected to the use of Welsh, the grace was then translated into Latin. Mansfield College adopted the Latin grace in 1953, with permission from U.C.N.W., Bangor.

> Hollalluog Dduw, Tad y trugareddau a ffynnon pob daioni: wrth fwynhau dy ddoniau bendigwn dy enw: trwy Iesu Grist ein Harglwydd: Amen.

> Omnipotens Deus Clementissime Pater omnis boni fons: in donis tuis gaudentes nomen tuum magnificamus: per Jesum Christum Dominum nostrum: Amen.

> Almighty God Father of mercies and fount of every good: in the enjoyment of thy gifts we bless thy name: through Jesus Christ our Lord: Amen.

> *Rev. Dr. John Marsh, who was Principal of*
> *Mansfield College when the grace came into use*

Ripon College, Oxford

Before the Meal

> *V.*   Whatever you do, in word or deed, do all in the name of the Lord Jesus.
> *R.*   Giving thanks to God the Father through him.
> *V.*   Bless O Lord this food to our use.
> *R.*   And ourselves to thy service. Amen.

After the Meal

    V.   For these and all his mercies God's holy name be
            blessed and praised.

    R.   Amen.

Rev. Canon D. P. Wilcox, Principal, Ripon College

Regent's Park College, Oxford

For the gifts of your grace
And the Fellowship of this College,
We praise your Name, O God.

Rev. B. R. White, Principal,
Regent's Park College

Ridley Hall, Cambridge

We thank thee O Lord for this food
but above all for the Living Bread
which comes down from heaven,
Jesus Christ, your Son, our Lord.

Rev. K. N. Sutton, Principal, Ridley Hall

Westcott House, Cambridge

A Translation of an Ancient Christian Grace

Blessed be God who gives food to all flesh, and has fed
us from our youth up until now. Fill our hearts, O
Lord, with joy and gladness, that always having all
that we need, we may have more than enough for every

good work in Christ Jesus our Lord, to whom with you and the Holy Spirit be all glory and praise, now and for ever. Amen.

Rev. Canon Mark Santer, Principal, Westcott House

Jews' College, London

Praised be the Lord our God
King of the World
He cares for the whole world.
With grace, loving kindness and mercy,
He gives food to all his creatures.
His goodness to us has been great
And we have never lacked for sustenance.
May he always provide for us
And may we never be in need of the
Gifts of flesh and blood. Amen.

N. L. Rabinovitch, Principal,
Jews' College

14

Family
&
Children

A Thought by **Robert Louis Stevenson**, 1850–94, from
A Child's Garden of Verse 1890.

> It is very nice to think
> The world is full of meat and drink,
> With little children saying grace
> In every Christian kind of place.

Rt. Rev. R. W. Heavener,
Bishop of Clogher

A Grace for Children by **Dr. Isaac Watts,** 1674–1748

Bless me, O Lord, and let my food strengthen me to
serve thee, for Jesus Christ's sake. Amen.

Graces from *A Child's Verse-Book of Devotion* 1840

> O Lord, I thank thee, who dost give
> The 'daily bread' by which I live;
> Oh! bless the food I now partake
> And save my soul for Jesus' sake.
>
> Before I take my pleasant food
> I'll thank the Lord, who is so good
> In sending all I need:
> Now Lord be pleased, I entreat,
> To bless the food that I may eat,
> And be my constant friend.

Thank you for the World so Sweet, by **E. Rutter Leatham.**

> Thank you for the world so sweet,
> Thank you for the food we eat.
> Thank you for the birds that sing,
> Thank you, God, for everything.

The Baby's Grace by **R. L. Gales.** This is more of a poem, although the last verse stands on its own as a grace. The last two lines have also been adapted to include such words as, 'For bacon, eggs and buttered toast, Praise Father, Son and Holy Ghost.'

> Baby's heart is lifted up
> For eggs laid into the cup.
> Yellow stained her praising lips
> With the bread and butter strips.
>
> Aged cripples by the bed
> Frugal feast on milk and bread,
> And the swarthy brigand men
> Eat risotto in their den.
>
> Praise to God who giveth meat
> Convenient unto all to eat:
> Praise for tea and buttered toast,
> Father, Son and Holy Ghost.

A Grace used by Canon Paul Gibson, when Principal of Ridley Hall, Cambridge.

> We ask a father's blessing on the children's food in Jesus' name.

Rt. Rev. J. V. Taylor, Bishop of Winchester

A Grace taught by the Rev. John Lawson, when a vicar in Shrewsbury in 1956. It appeared in a book of children's prayers, the author and title of which he cannot recall. He found that it was an appropriate grace for teaching godly *and* clean manners at table!

> Clean of hands and clean of face,
> I sit me down to say my grace,
> God bless the food that here we see,
> God bless you and God bless me.

Mrs. Phyllis Cormack

Our Daily Bread

> Bread is a lovely thing to eat—
> God bless the barley and the wheat;
> A lovely thing to breathe is air—
> God bless the sunshine everywhere;
> The earth's a lovely place to know—
> God bless the folks that come and go!
> Alive's a lovely thing to be—
> Giver of life—we say—bless thee!

It is significant that most of the graces that appear in print are for children. Here are some from various books of children's prayers.

A Book of Graces, from the Church of the Good Samaritan, Inyanga, Zimbabwe

> Thank you, God, for rain and sun,
> And all the plants that grow,
> Thank you for our daily food
> And friends who love us so.

From *The Infant Teacher's Prayer Book* by D. M. Prescott

> Thank you for the sunshine,
> Thank you for the rain,
> Thank you for the food we eat—
> We'll be thanking you again.

A Grace by Emilie Fendall Johnson in *A Little Book of Prayers*

> We thank thee, Lord, for happy hearts,
> For rain and sunny weather,
> We thank thee, Lord, for this our food,
> And that we are together.

A Winter Grace by Elfrida Vipont

> Dear Father, let the beasts and birds
> Be sheltered, safe and fed,
> And let me ne'er forget to share
> With them my daily bread.
>
> Help all the children everywhere
> Who hungry are and cold,
> And people who have lost their homes,
> And people who are old.

And may I grow up big and strong
And learn to help them too,
And work to make thy Kingdom come
When all thy Will shall do.

Rt. Rev. H. D. Halsey, Bishop of Carlisle

A Breakfast Grace, from *Start the Day Well* by Beryl Bye

We thank you Lord, for this good food. Be with us as
we eat it, and stay with each one of us throughout the
coming day. In your Name we ask it.

A Grace to be sung before tea

For all thy gifts we bless thee Lord,
But chiefly for our heavenly food—
Thy pardoning grace—
Thy quickening word—
These prompt our song
That God is good.

Mrs. M. Curtis

A Grace at Supper time

For rest and shelter of the night,
Father we thank thee.
For health and food, for love and friends,
Father, we thank thee.

Miss J. M. Crawford

Some Short Graces

A Grace 'At any time', by A. S. T. Fisher

> For every cup and plateful
> God make us truly grateful.

> Rub-a-dub-dub,
> thanks Lord for the grub.

> *Jim Scott, Scargill House*

> O Lord, make us able
> to eat the grub on this table.

> *Attributed to St. Mary Magdalene School,*
> *West Bromwich*

The Shortest Grace

> Heavenly Pa, ta!

> *Mrs. M. Curtis*

The Soul-Day Song

'Souling' was a custom in the North Midland counties of England, practised until the early years of the twentieth century. On All Souls' Day (November 2nd), the poor people would go from parish to parish soliciting money and specially prepared soul-cakes from the homes of the wealthy. In later years the custom seems to have been taken over by children, 'repeating certain rigmarole verses' and singing for cakes or money. The soul-day song probably originated from this practice, with the last line referring to the deeper significance of the festival.

> God bless the Master of this house
> And bless the Missus too
> And all the little children
> Around the table, too:
> Around the table, true good man,
> And happy may you be,
> Sing Father, Son and Holy Ghost
> And life eternally.

A Country House Grace. Mrs. E. M. Eastes' maternal grandmother was taught this grace in the 1870s, when she used to live at a country house in Fairford, Gloucestershire. The grace was said before the three main meals of the day and one can almost picture the smugness of the children on a cold winter's evening.

> Thank you, Lord, as we sit here,
> With feast and fire and nought to fear;
> Pity the unhappy poor—
> And bless this house for evermore.

A Family Grace, which the contributor remembers as being 'sung to a dirge', whilst the mutton cooled and the gravy congealed.

> Lord, for these and all thy mercies,
> Heartfelt thanks our lips out-pour,
> Day by day on us thou sendest,
> Blessings from thy countless store,
> Thine be all the praise and glory,
> Thine both now and evermore. Amen.

Mrs. D. (Findlay) Clayre

The Nantclwyd House Grace. A unique family grace has been carved around a large rectangular oak table at Nantclwyd House, Ruthin, North Wales, by the late Mr. Samuel Dyer-Gough. Nantclwyd House dates from the fourteenth century and is one of the finest houses in Ruthin. Until 1972, it was used as the residence of the Assize Judge when on circuit.

> Set thee down with cheerful face and happy mind to enjoy the fruit of thy labour.
>
> Labour not eat not saith Paul.
>
> Bless ye the Bountiful Goodness of thy God who provideth all food for body and soul.
>
> Thus thou shalt live in peace.

Mrs. S. Dyer-Gough

Family Graces, remembered by contributors when they were children, sometimes seventy or eighty years ago.

> Accept of our thanks O Heavenly Father, for this our food and every other blessing we receive at thy Bountiful hands, in the name of our Lord Jesus Christ. Amen.

Ms. Mary E. Corfield

> Our Gracious Father accept our thanks
> for these gifts of thy love.
> Grant us Thy richest blessing.
> Pardon every sin, for Christ's sake. Amen.

Oscar Evans

Grant us thy Blessing O Lord, and accept our thanks-givings for these and all thy mercies, for Jesus Christ's sake. Amen.

Miss Gysberta Winton Lewis

Gracious God we have sinned against thee, and are unworthy of thy mercy, pardon our sins and bless these mercies for our use, and help us to eat and drink to thy glory, for Jesus' sake. Amen.

Mrs. Mary McMurehy, who adds that this seemed a particularly long grace when she was a girl

Family Graces said in homes today

For families, friends
and this food, we thank God.

Rt. Rev. J. M. Bickersteth
Bishop of Bath and Wells

For the farmers who have worked that we may eat;
for those who have bought and sold this food;
for those who have prepared it;
and most of all to you, who planned it,
we thank you, God.

Rev. A. C. F. Nicoll

A Grace to be said in unison

For health,
For food,
And for the work of others,
We thank God.

Rt. Rev. R. O. Bowlby,
Bishop of Newcastle

15

Humorous & light-hearted Graces

An Old Rhyme

He that without grace sitteth down to eate,
Forgetting to give God thanks for his meate,
And riseth again letting grace surpasse,
Sitteth down like an oxe and riseth like an asse.

A Nursery Limerick

There was once a goose and a wren
Who gave lunch to a cock and a hen:
'O Lord' prayed the goose,
'Bless these gifts to our use
And ourselves in thy service. Amen.'

Hodge's Grace, probably dating from the time of the
agricultural distress in the nineteenth century.

Heavenly Father, bless us,
And keep us all alive;
There's ten of us to dinner
And not enough for five.

A Modern Variation

Three potatoes for four of us
Thank the Lord, there are no more of us!

D. MacInnes

O Bountiful Jehovah

The Rev. Sidney Smith, 1771–1845, that most delightful of clerics, is said to have always looked round to see if there was any champagne on the sideboard before saying grace. If there was, he would always begin with the words, 'O bountiful Jehovah'. If there was not, he would start, 'O Lord even for the least of these thy mercies . . .'

John Julius Norwich

Three Graces by Dean Swift, 1667–1745, the satirist who was always ready to challenge inequality and injustice. These graces indicate his great sense of humour.

A Grace uttered extempore after dinner with a miser

1 Thanks for this miracle! This is no less
   Than to eat manna in the wilderness.
   Where raging hunger reigned, we've found relief,
   And seen that wondrous thing, a piece of beef.
   Here chimneys smoke, that never smoked before,
   And we've all ate, where we shall eat no more.

A well-known traditional Grace has also been attributed to Swift

2 For rabbits young and rabbits old,
   For rabbits hot and rabbits cold,
   For rabbits tender, rabbits tough,
   We thank thee, Lord: we've had enough.

A Grace pronounced after breakfasting on bacon and eggs on a Friday at an Irish Monastery. The monks, of course, were having fish.

3   Does any man of common sense
    Think ham and eggs give God offence?
    Or that a herring has a charm
    The Almighty's anger to disarm?
    Wrapped in his majesty divine,
    D'you think he cares on what we dine?

A Modern Grace, mentioned by many contributors and attributed to the Very Rev. Lancelot Fleming, when Dean of Windsor.

O Lord grant that we may not be like porridge,
Stiff, stodgy and hard to stir,
But like cornflakes, crisp, fresh and ready to serve.

Be present at our table Lord
With guests we must but can't afford!
And let there be no strain or fuss
As if we always feasted thus.
And let the daily woman stay
Till half past two to clear away.

*Rt. Rev. K. E. N. Lamplugh, Honorary
Chaplain to Winchester Cathedral and
former Suffragan Bishop of Southampton
—he claims that he has never used the grace!*

A Confusion of Bishops. Both the Archbishop of Canterbury and the Archbishop of Wales visited Hawarden, in North Wales, for a ceremony connected with St. Deiniol's library. When a Bishop or Archbishop is present, his Chaplain normally says grace for him. On this occasion, each Chaplain thought that the other was going to say grace, which resulted in a long and embarrassing pause. Eventually the wife of the then Archbishop of Canterbury said:—

'It is a pity that two graces don't make a third!'

Sir William Gladstone, Bt., Chief Scout

A Slip of the Tongue. A new student—shy and of a slightly nervous disposition was asked to say the grace in the dining-hall of the theological college. The meal before him did not look especially appetizing. The following grace was offered unintentionally.

> We thank thee, dear Lord, for this food. Now we pray that thou wilt give us strength to eat it!

> *W. J. Arthur, Communications Director,*
> *Seventh-Day Adventist Church*

A Speaker's Grace, from *We Gather Together*

> O Lord, we thank you for this food we are privileged to eat and we beseech you to help us to speak the right words that we may not have to eat them later on.

> *Mrs. Sibyl Harton*

A Commercial Grace. An American T.V. announcer, who always introduced programmes as coming by courtesy of such and such a company, when asked to say grace unexpectedly at dinner, said:—

> 'This food comes to us by courtesy of Almighty God'.

> *Rt. Rev. R. A. S. Martineau, Bishop of Blackburn*

Grace after Pudding

Bishop Burroughs, from Zimbabwe, relates how his mother once said, 'I think we'll say grace after the meal—I am not sure how the pudding will turn out.'

A Benison on wartime high tea by Allan Laing.

Upon this scanty meal, O Lord,
Bestow a blessing in accord:
Pour thy grace in measure small,
Lest it more than cover all.

Bless the tiny piece of ham:
Bless the lonely dab of jam:
Bless the sparsely-buttered toast,
Father, Son and Holy Ghost.

Grace for the Comfortably Off, by Frances Russell.

God bless this food
Superfluous,
And may it put
No weight on us. Amen.

An Appreciative Grace

Thanks for breakfast, lunch and dinner,
If it weren't for you, I'd be much thinner.

J. Stubbs

A Victorian Grace?

I have had an elegant sufficiency of enoughness, any-
more would be an over-indulgence of my already
satisfied appetite.

Mrs. A. Rigby

Now, God be praised, we are not so poor as to lack meat for our stomachs nor so rich as to lack stomach for our meat.

Jessie and Eric Swan

A Grace from an American Placemat

God of goodness, bless our food.
Keep us in a pleasant mood.
Bless the cook and all who serve us.
From indigestion, Lord, preserve us. Amen.

A Grace used by the Rev. F. J. Dove, late past Master and former Honorary Chaplain of the Leathersellers' Company.

Whatever the weather
There's nothing like leather,
Whatever the mood
There's nothing like food,
Thanks be to God.

C. Davenport

A popular modern Grace, mentioned by several contributors, including the Rt. Rev. G. E. Reindorp, Bishop of Salisbury, whose four-year-old grand-daughter taught him the words!

God bless this bunch;
As we munch our lunch.

Bless these sinners as they eat their dinners.

J. Scott, Scargill House, N. Yorks.

Lord may we eat all we are able,
Until our stomachs touch the table.

Mrs. N. M. Barugh

Grace after a Meal

For bread and wine
And Auld Lang Syne:
God's holy Name be praised.

*Rev. L. E. M. Claxton, Rector of St. Olave's
and Chaplain to the Clothworkers' Company*

A Comment by Sir John Betjeman

For what we are about to receive the Lord make us
truly thankful.

'I think of it as a prelude to scraping of chairs, meat with
tubes in it such as is only found at school; and a prospect
of cold tapioca pudding before games in the afternoon.'

A Durham Miner's Grace. The following item occurred
in a copy of 'Notes and Queries' 1870. The writer, a clergyman, remembered his father telling him of a time when he
had occasion to visit a Durham miner in his tiny shack at
meal time—about 1800. When the clergyman's father
walked in, he found the miner and his family standing for
grace at their simple kitchen table, which was set with a

pot of soup, bread and some cheese. The miner bowed his head and said, reverently:—

'What we're about to receive has nowt to do wi' the Duke of Newcastle.'

Frank Muir

This should be contrasted with the opposite sentiment, in the following grace.

God bless the squire and his relations,
And help us know our proper stations.

Mrs. Grace Close

A Headmaster's Grace, attributed to Geoffrey Fisher, former Archbishop of Canterbury, when headmaster of Repton.

For what we are about to receive and for what some have already snatched, may the Lord make us truly thankful.

Rev. L. G. Tyler

A Sailor's Grace, attributed to a former Bishop of Winchester.

For what we are about to receive and for what we are permitted to retain, may the Lord make us truly thankful.

Rev. L. G. Tyler

A Lawyer's Grace

For whom we are about to deceive, may the Lord make us truly thankful.

Dr. G. K. Mackenzie

A Musician's Grace. After sorting out some of his financial difficulties, in 1924 Sir Thomas Beecham, 1879–1961, was in a position to discharge enough of his personal debts to satisfy the Official Receiver.

'For what he is about to receive,' said Beecham, 'may the Lord make him truly thankful.'

16

Favourite Graces

Derek Nimmo, the actor, often uses this simple grace.

> For food and health and hope, we thank you Lord. Give us also a sensitive heart and a generous hand to share these gifts with others. Amen.

A Favourite Grace from the late Joyce Grenfell, writer, actress and comedienne. The Headmaster of Lancing College, Mr. I. Beer, has a similar grace, and adds that meals should be occasions when friends are made and friendships grow.

> For Good Food,
> and Good Friends,
> Thank God.

David Jacobs, the broadcaster, has the following grace, because it is unpompous, brief and to the point.

> For this and us, God bless.

A Grace from the actress, Judi Dench

> For our food and those who have prepared it, we thank God.

Lord Hunt, leader of the first team to conquer Everest, says this grace at formal dinners. It represents his feeling that a happy life depends upon an attitude of thankfulness and love.

> For food and fellowship,
> Thank God.

Bishop Kenneth Lamplugh, Honorary Chaplain to Winchester Cathedral and a former Suffragan Bishop of Southampton, has used his grace for the past twenty-five years and is always being asked for it.

> For food we eat, and those who prepare it,
> For health to enjoy it and friends to share it.
> We thank thee O Lord. Amen.

A Favourite Grace from the Rt. Rev. G. E. Reindorp, Bishop of Salisbury.

> Christ in the wilderness—5000 fed:
> Two small fishes and five loaves of bread.
> May the blessing of him,
> Who made the division:
> Rest upon us,
> And upon our provision.

Canon L. J. Collins, Canon of St. Pauls, author and former Dean of Oriel College, Oxford, believes that his favourite grace is derived from an old naval grace.

> For food and drink and fellowship,
> God's holy name be praised.

The Rt. Rev. S. W. Phipps, Bishop of Lincoln, quotes the words of a former Bishop of Lincoln, St. Hugh 1135–1200, who rebuilt the greater part of Lincoln cathedral and was known for his liberality to the poor and lepers.

> Eat well and drink well,
> and serve God well and devoutly.

Finally, the **Rt. Rev. Hugh Montefiore, Bishop of Birmingham** adds:

Thank you God for our lovely food!

17

The Bible

There is evidence of saying grace in the Old Testament, illustrating the development of this form of thanksgiving. Many graces are taken from the Psalms and in the New Testament, Jesus prefaced a meal with thanks, at the feeding of the 4,000 and 5,000 and at the Last Supper.

Exodus Chap. 18 v. 12

And Jethro, Moses' father in law, took a burnt offering and sacrifices for God: and Aaron came, and all the elders of Israel, to eat bread with Moses' father in law before God.

Exodus Chap. 23 v. 25

And ye shall serve the Lord your God, and he shall bless thy bread, and thy water.

Deuteronomy Chap. 8 v. 10

When thou hast eaten and art full, then thou shalt bless the Lord thy God for the good land which he hath given thee.

1 Samuel Chap. 9 v. 13. Samuel has to bless the meal before the people can eat.

As soon as ye be come into the city, ye shall straightway find him, before he go up to the high place to eat: for the people will not eat until he come, because he doth bless the sacrifice; and afterwards they eat that be bidden.

1 Chronicles Chap. 29 v. 13

Now therefore, our God, we thank thee, and praise thy
glorious name.

Psalm 68 v. 19

Blessed be the Lord, who daily loadeth us with benefits,
even the God of our salvation.

Psalm 92 v. 1

It is a good thing to give thanks unto the Lord.

The Rt. Rev. David Sheppard, Bishop of Liverpool,
suggests the following grace, from **Psalm 103 v. 2.**

Bless the Lord, O my soul, and forget not all his benefits.

The Fearon Grace, from **Psalm 145 v. 15 and 16,** was
used in the old monastic form of service and is still said by
many religious communities today.

The eyes of all wait upon thee; and thou givest them
their meat in due season.

Thou openest thine hand, and satisfiest the desire of
every living thing.

St. Matthew Chap. 4 v. 4.

Man shall not live by bread alone, but by every word that proceedeth out of the mouth of God.

St. Matthew Chap. 26 v. 26 and 27. The Last Supper

And as they were eating, Jesus took bread, and blessed it, and brake it, and gave it to the disciples, and said, Take, eat; this is my body.

And he took the cup, and gave thanks, and gave it to them, saying, Drink ye all of it.

St. Luke Chap. 11 v. 3

Give us day by day our daily bread.

St. John Chap. 6. v. 11. The feeding of the five thousand

And Jesus took the loaves; and when he had given thanks, he distributed to the disciples, and the disciples to them that were set down; and likewise of the fishes as much as they would.

And when he had thus spoken, he took bread, and gave thanks to God in presence of them all: and when he had broken it, he began to eat.

1 Corinthians Chap. 10 v. 31

Whether therefore ye eat, or drink, or whatsoever ye do, do all to the glory of God.

1 Thessalonians Chap. 5 v. 18

In every thing give thanks: for this is the will of God in Christ Jesus concerning you.

1 Timothy Chap. 4 v. 3-5

God hath created (meat) to be received with thanksgiving of them which believe and know the truth.

For every creature of God is good, and nothing to be refused, if it be received with thanksgiving:

For it is sanctified by the word of God and prayer.

1 Timothy Chap. 6 v. 17

. . . nor trust in uncertain riches, but in the living God, who giveth us richly all things to enjoy.

18

General Graces
&
Prayers

The Johnny Appleseed Grace. Johnny Appleseed, or John Chapman 1774–1845, was an American pioneer and folk hero. He went to the Pennsylvanian frontier in 1797 and established orchards in his wanderings. His altruism was unusual in the days when people were often only seeking to procure land for themselves. As a Swedenborgian, he became a missionary for that philosophy. The grace is a particular favourite with the Guides and Brownies.

> The Lord is good to me,
> And so I thank the Lord
> For giving me the things I need,
> The sun, the rain, and the appleseed.
> The Lord is good to me.
>
> And every seed that grows
> Will grow into a tree.
> And one day soon
> There'll be apples there,
> For everyone in the world to share,
> The Lord is good to me.

The Wayfarer's Grace by **M. Elizabeth Worsfold**

> For all the glory of the way,
> For thy protection night and day,
> For roof-tree, fire, and bed and board,
> For friends and home, we thank thee, Lord.

A Refectory Grace from Chester Cathedral, written by Thomas Henry Basil Webb, born on August 12th, 1898 and educated at Winchester College—he was killed on the Somme, December 1st, 1917, aged nineteen. The grace is no longer used at the Cathedral.

> Give me a good digestion, Lord,
> And also something to digest;
> But when and how that something comes
> I leave to thee, who knowest best.

A Grace before a Meal, by **the Rev. Canon J. W. Poole,** who adds that the Latin word 'gratia' also means liking, charm and kindness and these words were in his mind when he composed the grace.

> Grace at this table,
> grace in our hearts,
> and grace in our homes,
> for Christ's sake. Amen.

A Grace attributed to Prince Albert, the Prince Consort, 1819–61

God bless our going out, nor less our coming in, and make them sure.
God bless our daily bread, and bless whate'er we do whate'er endure.
In death until his peace awake us,
And heirs of his salvation make us.

A Grace by Avery Brooke

Father, we thank you for this meal,
for our lives,
for other people,
for beautiful things,
for goodness and for you.

All we have comes from you, O loving Father:
Help us to be more and more aware of your goodness to us.

Mrs. J. Pickard, former Headmistress,
The Mount School, York

For all this, so much more than daily bread,
Accept our grateful thanks, O Lord.

Jessie and Eric Swan

A Grace by Sister Mary Teresa

Let love be the sweetness and wisdom the seasoning at this table, O heavenly Father. Amen.

Dear Lord, your mercies are new every morning; great is your faithfulness. Accept our grateful thanks for every provision for all our needs, especially for this food now before us: please use it to strengthen our bodies, and use our bodies in your service. For Jesus Christ's sake. Amen.

Rev. David H. Wheaton, Honorary Canon of St. Albans

For healthy appetites,
good food and pleasant company,
we thank you O God.

Tom Houston,
Executive Director, Bible Society

For these and all thy gifts,
we praise thy name, O Lord.

Miss V. Fraser, Headmistress,
The Godolphin School

Finally, **A. J. P. Taylor, the historian,** recalls how the economist, **G. D. H. Cole,** an atheist, used to stand with lips firmly sealed during the saying of grace and then shuffle his chair as a signal to sit down!

May the grace of Christ our Saviour,
And the Father's boundless love,
With the Holy Spirit's favour,
Rest upon us from above.

Rev. John Newton, 1725–1807
A wandering sea captain and slave trader
who later became an evangelical clergyman.
He collaborated with Cowper in the Olney Hymns, 1779

ACKNOWLEDGMENTS

The compiler and the publishers are grateful to the following for permission to include graces in this anthology:

Blandford Press, for the grace 'Thank you for the sunshine...', from *The Infant Teacher's Prayer Book* by D. M. Prescott.

Jonathan Cape Ltd., The Executors of the James Joyce Estate, The Society of Authors, and Viking Penguin Inc., for a grace from *A Portrait of the Artist as a Young Man* by James Joyce. Copyright 1916 by B. W. Huebsch, renewed 1944 by Nora Joyce.

William Collins Sons & Co. Ltd., for a grace from *Plain Prayers for a Complicated World* by Avery Brooke; for a grace from *Fame is the Spur* by Howard Spring; and a grace from *A Book of Prayers for Children* by Elfrida Vipont.

William Collins Sons & Co. Ltd. (Fontana), for graces from *More Prayers for Women* by Rita Snowden.

Evans Brothers Ltd., for the grace 'Bread is a lovely thing to eat', from *Prayers for Child Education* by A. W. L. Chitty and Mary Osborn.

A. S. T. Fisher, for a grace from *An Anthology of Prayers* by A. S. T. Fisher.

Victor Gollancz Ltd., for a grace from *Pastors and Masters* by I. Compton-Burnett.

Hodder & Stoughton Ltd., for graces from *Uncommon Prayers* by Cecil Hunt.

J. D. Lewis & Sons Ltd., Gomer Press, for a grace by W. D. Williams, Barmouth.

Lion Publishing, for 'A Prayer from China', from *The Lion Book of Children's Prayers* by Mary Batchelor.

Lutterworth Press, for the grace 'We thank you Lord, for this good food . . .', from *Start the Day Well* by Beryl Bye.

Paulist Press, New York, for graces from *Prayers at Mealtime* by Sister Mary Teresa OP.

Routledge & Kegan Paul Ltd., and the Reverend Jiyu Kennett, for prayers from *Selling Water by the River* by the Reverend Jiyu Kennett.

Routledge & Kegan Paul Ltd., and Shambhala Publications Inc., for the Vimalakirti Sutra from *Selling Water by the River* by the Reverend Jiyu Kennett and from *The Vimalakirti Sutra*, translated and edited by Charles Luk. Copyright 1972 by Charles Luk.

The Seabury Press Inc., for graces from *We Gather Together: A Cookbook of Recipes by the Wives of the Bishops of the Episcopal Church*. Copyright © 1976 by The Seabury Press Inc.

Acknowledgment is also made to the following copyright holders who have not been traced:

Mrs. Lorna Hill, for 'Thank you for the world so sweet' by E. Rutter Leatham.

Emilie Fendall Johnson, for 'We thank thee, Lord, for happy hearts' from *A Little Book of Prayers* by Emilie Fendall Johnson.

Allan Laing for 'A Benison on wartime tea' from *Bank Holiday on Parnassus* by Allan Laing.

In addition, grateful acknowledgment is made to the many correspondents for allowing their graces to be included in this collection, the Clerks of the London Livery Companies, the Deacon Convener, Trinity Hall, Aberdeen, the Oxford and Cambridge Colleges for permission to use their graces, the four Inns of Court—Gray's Inn, Inner Temple, Lincoln's Inn and the Middle Temple—the Warden and Fellows of Winchester College and the Headmasters of the other schools whose graces have been included, Mrs. Owen Walker, The Chief Commissioner, The Girl Guides Association, for permission to use the Guide and Brownie graces and Mrs. Alicia Horsfall for graces from *A Book of Graces* from the Church of the Good Samaritan, Inyanga, Zimbabwe.

As well as translations from contributors, gratitude is expressed for the valuable help received from Mrs. P. Rae for the French translations, Mrs. J. Jackson for the German translations and Mrs. E. Edmunds for the Welsh translations.

INDEX OF SOURCES

Contributors have been included in this index when authors of a grace.

INDEX OF FIRST PHRASES

209